Dynamic Presentations

Michael Hood

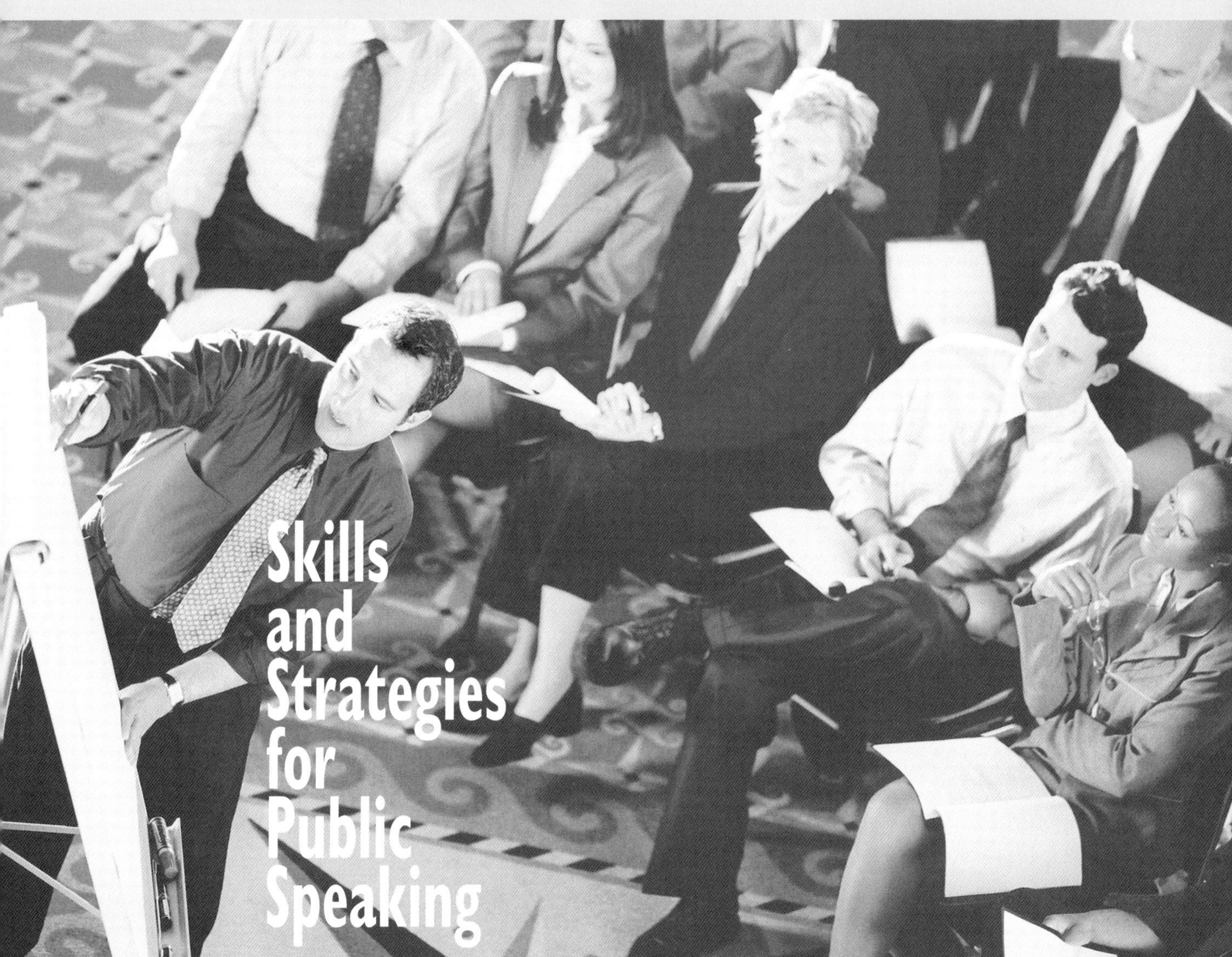

KINSEIDO

Kinseido Publishing Co., Ltd.
3-21 Kanda Jimbo-cho, Chiyoda-ku,
Tokyo 101-0051, Japan

Design: parastyle inc.
Illustrations: Junji Aoki

[Photo Credits]
p. 31-5 Yomiuri Shimbun
p. 37 Sally Dillon / Lonely Planet Images
p. 39 Kim Grant / Lonely Planet Images
p. 43 Yomiuri Shimbun
p. 45 Darren Staples / Reuter-Sun
p. 49 Yomiuri Shimbun
pp. 61, 63 Yomiuri Shimbun

音声ファイル無料ダウンロード

http://www.kinsei-do.co.jp/download/4156

この教科書で DL 00 の表示がある箇所の音声は、上記 URL または QR コードにて無料でダウンロードできます。自習用音声としてご活用ください。

- ▶ PC からのダウンロードをお勧めします。スマートフォンなどでダウンロードされる場合は、**ダウンロード前に「解凍アプリ」をインストール**してください。
- ▶ URL は、**検索ボックスではなくアドレスバー（URL 表示欄）**に入力してください。
- ▶ お使いのネットワーク環境によっては、ダウンロードできない場合があります。

CD 00 左記の表示がある箇所の音声は、教室用 CD（Class Audio CD）に収録されています。

Introduction

Dynamic Presentations: Skills and Strategies for Public Speaking empowers students with voice. Employing a communicative, task-based approach, this course provides the tools, experience, and ultimately the confidence students need to present their own ideas clearly and effectively—in real-life contexts for various authentic purposes.

A Communicative & Task-Based Approach

This text is premised on the idea that students learn English most effectively by using it to complete meaningful tasks. Each unit presents students with the opportunity to make a presentation for an authentic purpose—the sorts of speaking tasks they may indeed be called upon to perform in the future. Drawing on their own interests, experience, and beliefs, students invest the presentations with meaning. At all stages of preparation and performance, students use English. Thus English is not *taught* as an abstraction; rather, it is *used* as a means to a meaningful and interesting end. In this way, all four skills (reading, writing, listening, and speaking) are developed throughout the course.

A Student-Centered Classroom

Activities are designed to give students as many opportunities to use English as possible. Students work in pairs or in groups to learn and practice skills and strategies. They review and critique each other's work as they create presentations, and they evaluate each other's performances. The teacher's primary role is to introduce and explain new concepts and direct activities. Then, as students work, the teacher assumes new roles—coach, model, and advisor—helping individuals as they encounter difficulty and keeping everyone on task. Students are given more control over their own learning, and they gain valuable experience using English and negotiating among their peers.

Critical Thinking

Given control over their own learning, students are challenged to think independently and critically—a skill that is developed not through explicit instruction but through frequent practice asking and answering critical questions. Early in this course, students make decisions about content, organization, and the needs of their audience. Later on, they learn to support and defend positions, evaluate reasons and evidence, and anticipate questions. Throughout this course, students identify strengths and weaknesses in their classmates' presentations, and they are challenged to think about and articulate their own views on various issues. All of these activities serve to develop students' critical thinking skills.

Content

Communication Skills. Each unit introduces a new communication skill. These are carefully sequenced, beginning with relatively easy non-verbal communication skills and proceeding to voice control skills. Beginning with Unit 9, rhetorical skills are introduced. In Units 13 and 14, students learn about different types of appeals. The final units show students how to conclude their speeches and answer questions. Together, these skills promote effective speech delivery. By the end of the course, students have a wide variety of communication skills to draw upon for public speaking.

Speech Building Strategies. Each unit also introduces a new speech building strategy. These are tools that help students generate details, find, evaluate, and organize information, and develop and support ideas. Whereas the communication skills are focused on delivery, the speech building strategies are focused on content. In most units, the building strategy is first introduced in the warm-up activity then presented more explicitly later. Speech building strategies range from simple outlining to creating and using visual aids. Later units introduce basic research strategies.

Performance & Purpose. Once new skills and strategies are learned and practiced through pair and group work, students incorporate them into formal presentations. Students are guided as they prepare their presentations, and they practice with a partner before performance. Each performance is defined by both general and specific purposes. Four broad and progressively more sophisticated purposes—describing, informing, explaining, and persuading—are practiced throughout the course. More specific and practical purposes inform individual presentations. Students begin by describing people and places and progress to informing about events. In later units, students explain processes and relationships and finally argue for solutions and policies. Presentations are modeled on the online videos.

Sound Pronunciation. This section uses minimal pairs to present and practice basic English pronunciation. Emphasis is placed on recognition of the phonetic symbols students are most likely to encounter in their dictionaries so that they can discern the pronunciation of new words.

Stress for Meaning & Clarity. Conventions of stress, intonation, pitch, and articulation are presented and practiced with an emphasis on how these conventions may affect meaning.

Grammar Review. The communicative approach holds that grammar is best learned through use. The grammar review section reinforces discrete grammatical points that were used earlier in the unit and may be useful to students as they write their presentations.

Video. Sixteen example presentations performed by native English speakers are included. These examples demonstrate the communication skills and speech building strategies introduced in the corresponding unit. The teacher's manual includes photocopiable handouts for analysis and discussion of each model demonstration.

Useful Expressions & Vocabulary. An appendix at the back of the book includes conventional expressions that students might use in their presentations. Also, new and important vocabulary words that were introduced in each unit are presented in quiz-form.

Flexibility

This text can be adapted to accommodate three variables—student level, class size, and the amount of time available for instruction. Teachers working with lower level students may choose to work more slowly and focus on the early units, which require less language production. Teachers of more advanced students may choose to move through the early units rapidly, spending more time on the later, more complex units. Teachers dealing with large classes may choose to have students perform their presentations in small groups; in smaller classes, all students can perform for the entire class. In either case, classmates evaluate performance (evaluation forms are included in early units; photocopiable forms are provided in the teacher's manual for later units).

Each unit is designed to be completed in two 90-minute class meetings, depending on the amount of time spent on performance. The entire text can be covered in two 14-week terms. However, the most important points can be covered in one term. In such cases, teachers must carefully select the most important activities appropriate for their students and reduce the number of performances. The teacher's manual includes additional guidance for completing the course in one term.

Support

The teacher's manual provides timeframes and guidance for each activity. Photocopiable evaluation forms, handouts for video exercises, tapescripts, answer keys, and supplemental activities are also included.

Final Thoughts

In the broadest sense, the purpose of this textbook is to empower students of English to investigate, articulate, and share their ideas about the world. By creating a classroom atmosphere in which students are encouraged to explore and express ideas, teachers can ensure that this course is a rich and rewarding experience for all. Good luck, and have fun!

Michael Hood

Contents

Unit 1

Good Speeches, Good Speakers

Warm-Up

Will you make many speeches in your life? Put a check (✓) next to the situations in which you may someday make a speech.

- ☐ A business meeting.
- ☐ A wedding reception.
- ☐ A job interview.
- ☐ A policy discussion.
- ☐ A lecture.
- ☐ A club meeting.
- ☐ A graduation ceremony.
- ☐ A memorial.

Speech Key 1.1

You will probably make many speeches in your life. The skills you learn in this course will help you perform all of them better.

Speech Key 1.2

Great speakers aren't born, they are made. Anyone can learn the skills. And with practice, you can become a great speaker!

What are the features of a good speech? What about good speakers?

Good Speakers	Good Speeches
well-prepared	*easy to understand*
______________	______________
______________	______________
______________	______________
______________	______________

Now check with a partner and compare your lists.

Before You Start: Understanding Your Purpose

When you are asked to make a speech, think about the purpose. Why are you giving the speech? What is your goal? Your answer will help you make important decisions about how to make your speech. Match the speech context on the left with the purpose on the right.

Speech Key 1.3

Remember your purpose! It will help you make important decisions as you build your speech.

1. You are making a speech at your best friend's wedding.
2. You are a salesman making a presentation to buyers.
3. You are a scientist presenting your latest discovery at a conference.
4. You are a company president making an annual report to shareholders.

a. explain
b. inform
c. entertain
d. persuade

Practice

Listen to the CD. You will hear the opening statements of some speeches. Can you identify the purpose? Write "I" if the purpose is to inform, "P" to persuade, "E" to entertain or "EX" to explain.

1. ____ 6. ____
2. ____ 7. ____
3. ____ 8. ____
4. ____ 9. ____
5. ____ 10. ____

Speech Key 1.4

In a good speech, the purpose is clear from the very beginning.

Building Your Speech: Outlining

An outline is like a map of your speech. It helps you organize your speech content clearly. It can also help you remember key points.

Example Outline

Purpose: Inform the audience about myself (self-introduction)

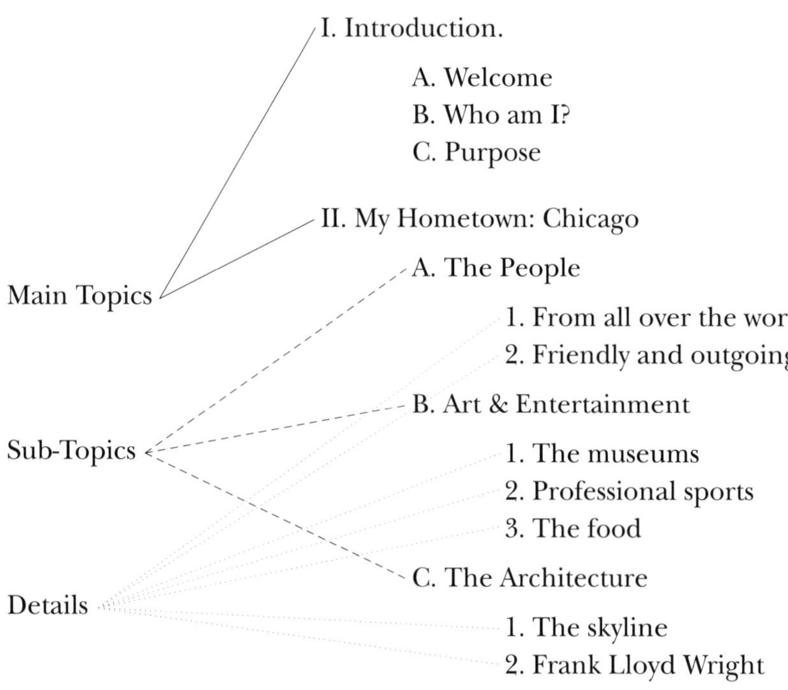

I. Introduction.
  A. Welcome
  B. Who am I?
  C. Purpose

II. My Hometown: Chicago
  A. The People
    1. From all over the world
    2. Friendly and outgoing
  B. Art & Entertainment
    1. The museums
    2. Professional sports
    3. The food
  C. The Architecture
    1. The skyline
    2. Frank Lloyd Wright

III. Conclusion
  A. Please visit
  B. Thank you
  C. Questions

How to Make an Outline

1. Think about the main topics of your speech. Put a number to the left of each one.
2. For each main topic, write all of the sub-topics. Put a capital letter next to the left of each one.
3. Under each sub-topic, write the key point or detail that you remember. Put a number to the left of each one.

Speech Key 1.5

A good outline will keep your information organized and help you remember key points.

Now listen to the CD and read the outline of Mike's self-introduction. Try to follow as he goes from main topic to sub-topic to details.

Practice

Now practice making an outline. Fill in the outline with the information in the box.

Cycling
Bachelor course
At Colorado State University
My bicycle trips
Their jobs
My brother, Bryan
Playing guitar
Their home in Atlanta
At the University of Illinois
Major: English
My parents
Master's course
Family
Hobbies
His family
My special bicycle
The type of music I play
Thesis: Literature
My special guitar
His job
Education

I. *Education*
  A. ______
    1. ______
    2. ______
  B. ______
    1. ______
    2. ______
II. ______
  A. ______
    1. ______
    2. ______
  B. ______
    1. *My special guitar*
    2. ______
III. ______
  A. *My parents*
    1. ______
    2. ______
  B. ______
    1. ______
    2. ______

Now listen to the CD and check your answers.

DL 04
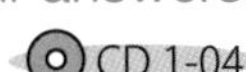
CD 1-04

Using a Dictionary

When you prepare your speech, use the English you already know. Don't try to communicate above your English level—it will be too difficult to speak naturally. However, you may want to use a few new words, so you will need to know how to use a dictionary effectively.

Using a Dictionary Effectively

1. Think of the idea in your native language.
2. Look for the word in a bilingual dictionary.
3. Search the entry for the information you need.

Example Dictionary Entry

Entry in an English-English Dictionary:

Pronunciation and stress (see key on page 6)
Part of speech
Definition

el·o·quent (éləkwənt), adj. 1. skilled in fluent, forceful, and appropriate speech.

English word, broken into syllables

Why Use a Dictionary?

1. To check spelling.
2. To check pronunciation.
3. To check meaning.
4. To find other words with the same meaning.

Practice

Let's practice using a dictionary. Work with a partner and look up the following words. Write down the correct pronunciation and stress, part of speech, and meaning.

Parts of Speech

n = noun	adv = adverb
v = verb	prep = preposition
adj = adjective	conj = conjunction

	pronunciation and stress	part of speech	meaning
1. prepare	______	______	______
2. organize	______	______	______
3. context	______	______	______
4. collaborate	______	______	______
5. definition	______	______	______

Now listen to the CD and practice saying these new words. 

CD 1-05

Working in Pairs & Groups

Throughout this course, you will work with a partner (in a pair) or with several other people (in a group). It is important to know how to work effectively in these contexts.

Why Work in Pairs or Groups?

✓ Get new ideas from your classmates.
✓ Share your own ideas with others.
✓ Have more chances to communicate.
✓ Make new friends.
✓ Share the work so it is easier.
✓ Learn together.
✓ Have fun!

Roles for Group Members

✓ Moderator: This person leads the group and makes sure everyone gets to speak.
✓ Recorder: This person takes notes about what is said in the group.
✓ Reporter: This person reports the results of the group work to the class.

Five Simple Rules for Effective Group Work

1. Take turns speaking, so everyone has a chance.
2. Listen carefully to what your classmates say.
3. Respond politely to the ideas of others.
4. Stay on the topic.
5. Make an effort to communicate in English only!

Practice

Now form a group of four or five. Appoint a moderator, recorder, and reporter. Return to the first page of this unit and:

1. Try to think of more situations in which you might make a speech in the future.
2. Brainstorm qualities of good speeches and good speakers.

Work for 15 minutes, then report your results to the class.

Sound Pronunciation

English letters can be pronounced in many ways. In your dictionary, you will find symbols for different sounds. We will practice these sounds throughout this course. You may refer to this symbol key chart at any time.

Vowel Sounds

symbol	example	symbol	example	symbol	example
i:	sleep	ɔ:	fall	ɔi	toy
i	flip	u	hook	au	mouse
e	hen	u:	shoot	ou	clone
æ	fan	ə:r	swirl	iə	fear
ʌ	fun	ei	fail	eə	hair
ɑ:	cart	ə	opera	u	hook
ɑ	cot	ai	wine		

Consonant Sounds

symbol	example	symbol	example
ʃ	she	r	right
ʒ	Asia	r	sure
tʃ	cheese		
dʒ	jewel		
θ	thick		
l	low		
l	tell		

Listen to the CD and repeat. 

Stress Patterns & Intonation

In English, stress can greatly effect the meaning of a sentence. Listen to the CD and read these examples. DL 07 CD 1-07

1. Oh, you bought a BIG house. (not a small one)
2. Oh, you bought a big HOUSE. (not a big car or a big boat)
3. Oh, you BOUGHT a big house. (you didn't rent or sell a big house)

▶ In each sentence, the heavy stress indicates the point that surprised the speaker. The stress carries meaning that the words do not.

Intonation can also effect the meaning. Listen to the CD and read these examples. DL 08 CD 1-08

1. You've had enough to eat. ⟶
2. You've had enough to eat? ↗

▶ In the second sentence, the intonation rises at the end. This means that the speaker is asking a question, even if the form of the sentence isn't a question (Have you had enough to eat?).

▶ In each unit, you will learn new stress and intonation patterns to help you make your speeches sound more natural.

Grammar Review: Simple Present Verb Form

The simple present verb form is to show action that is usual or habitual; something that is true now and is always or usually true.

Form	be	other verbs	Use
I	am	play	Ex. I live in Tokyo.
You/We/They	are	play	They study every day.
He/She/It	is	plays	She lives in New York.
			He studies early in the morning.

* Notice the final -s added to the 3rd person singular.

** Sometimes the final -y is changed to -ie.
Ex. study▸studies, marry▸marries

Fill in each blank with a verb from the box. Write the verb in the correct form.

1. Jeremy ______________ baseball every Saturday afternoon.
2. He ______________ of becoming a professional player someday.
3. My mother and father ______________ waffles with strawberries for breakfast.
4. It ______________ cold in here. Please turn up the heat.
5. Children ______________ languages much faster than older people.
6. My brother ______________ a lot of money at his new job.
7. He ______________ to different cities on business.
8. I ______________ about 5 books every month.
9. Carrie ______________ a new car.
10. Ken ______________ in the ocean in summer.

eat
dream
want
play
make
feel
swim
fly
read
learn

Compare your answers with a partner. Then listen to the CD and check. DL 09 CD 1-09

Unit 2

Introduce Yourself!

Warm-Up

In both presentations and conversations, it is important to introduce yourself.

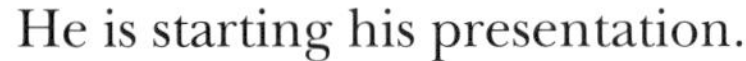

He is starting his presentation.

They are shaking hands.

In both pictures, these people are introducing themselves. We introduce ourselves in conversations and in presentations and speeches. How are these introductions the same? How are they different? Work with a partner and write "C" for parts of a conversation and "S" for parts of a speech. Write "B" for both.

____ Shake hands.
____ Use a microphone.
____ Speak to many people.
____ Talk about yourself.

____ Make eye contact.
____ Speak to one person.
____ Take turns talking.
____ Use gestures.

Speech Key 2.1

Like a conversation, a speech is communication. But you share information with more than one person.

Speech Skill: Eye Contact

When you have a conversation, you usually make eye contact with your partner. This helps you communicate. The same is true for a speech. Follow these steps to make eye contact during a speech.

Eye Contact During a Speech

1. Make eye contact with someone.
2. Hold eye contact for one or two seconds.
3. Break eye contact.
4. Repeat with another person.

Troubleshooting

In the first picture, the speaker is making good eye contact. The other pictures show him making common mistakes. Work with a partner and write a short sentence to explain the mistake. Use the verbs below.

Speech Key 2.2

You cannot read and make eye contact at the same time. Know your speech content very well, so you don't need to read.

think	read	look past

1. *He's making eye contact.* 2. ________ 3. ________ 4. ________

Practice

Listen to the CD. The speaker is making a self-introduction speech. What do you learn about him? In the space below, write the topics and details you hear. DL 10 CD 1-10

What Did You Learn about Mike?

topic	detail
Teaching experience	*literature*

When you introduce yourself, what should you tell your audience? Work with a partner and make a list of topics to include in a self-introduction. Then share your ideas with the class. Write down any new ideas you learn from your classmates.

Interesting Topics for a Self-introduction

Hobbies

Building Your Speech: Introduction

A good speech starts with some basic information. This prepares people to listen.

Parts of a Speech Introduction

1. Make a greeting. This announces the start of the speech. You can also thank the audience for coming.
2. Identify yourself. Give your name and position or title. The audience needs to know who is speaking.
3. Explain the purpose of the speech. The audience needs to know why you are talking to them.
4. Preview the speech. Tell your audience the topics you will talk about in your speech.
5. Tell your audience how much time you will take.

Put the correct number of the speech introduction part (1, 2, 3, 4, or 5) in the space next to each statement. The first one is done for you.

_2_ My name is Bob Jones, President of IBI Company.
____ I will take just a few minutes of your time.
____ Ladies and Gentlemen, thank you for coming.
____ Today I would like to tell you about our company.
____ I will explain our products, services, and future plans.
____ I would like to take a few minutes to introduce myself.
____ Good afternoon everyone. I'm very happy to see you.
____ I'm David Smith, a third-year student.
____ I will speak to you for about five minutes.
____ I will tell you a little about my hobbies, school life, and career goals.

Practice

These are statements from Jessica's self-introduction. But they are out of order! Number them in the correct order from 1 to 13. The first one has been done for you.

____ First, my favorite hobby is photography.
____ My name is Jessica Davis. I'm the President of Speech Masters.
____ Thank you for listening today. Do you have any questions?
____ Finally, let me explain why I joined Speech Masters.
____ I have two older brothers and two older sisters.
_1_ Good afternoon, ladies and gentlemen. Thank you for coming today.
____ So I am the youngest child.
____ I started taking pictures when I was in elementary school.
____ I would like to tell you a little about myself.
____ Second, I have a large family.
____ To be an excellent public speaker, you need to practice.
____ I will tell you about my hobby, my family, and my reasons for joining Speech Masters.
____ Speech Masters gives me the chance to practice and develop my skills as a public speaker.

Compare your answers with a partner. Now listen to the CD and check.

DL 11 CD 1-11

Prepare

Take about ten minutes and write a short (2–3 minutes) self-introduction in the space below. Think about what your audience should know about you. Include a speech introduction. Refer to the topics listed on page 8.

Self-Introduction

____

____

____

____

____

____

____

Practice

Now practice your speech with a partner. Help your partner improve the speech by making a list of his/her strengths and weaknesses. Also, write one or two questions for your partner.

Notes on Your Partner's Speech

Strengths ______________________________

____

Weaknesses ______________________________

____

Questions ______________________________

____

Take turns and practice your speech as many times as possible.

Speech Key 2.3

Practice! Practice! Practice! Even the best speakers rehearse their speeches many times before they perform.

Perform

Perform your self-introduction for the class or in small groups. Remember to make eye contact with different members of your audience.

Speech Key 2.4

Think about your audience! Who are you communicating with? Why are they listening to you? What do they need to know? What do they want to know?

Evaluation

As your classmates perform their self-introductions, listen and watch carefully. Follow the example below, and fill in the evaluation chart.

Name	Good eye contact	Reading	Looking up	Looking past the audience	Comments
Kenji Taguchi	*||||*	*|||*	*|*	*||*	*Good, but did not explain purpose.*

Sound Pronunciation

Let's practice long and short vowel sounds.

[i:] This is a long vowel sound.
 feel, see, read, keep, eat, need, sheet

[i] This is a short vowel sound.
 fill, will, sit, lick, stick, win, ship

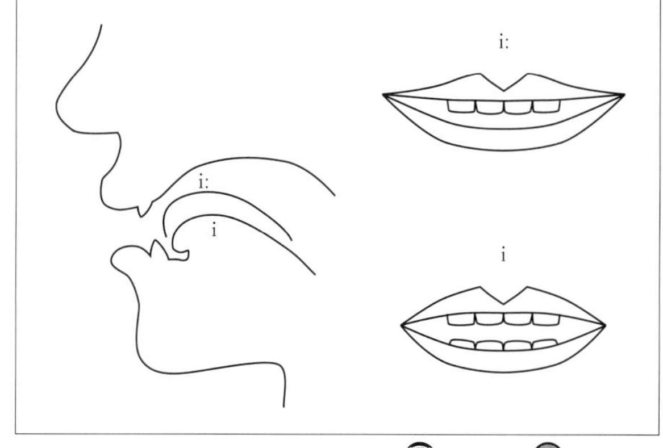

Now, listen to the CD DL 12 CD 1-12 and repeat.

DL 13 CD 1-13

Write "i:" or "i" on the line to describe the vowel sound. Then listen to the CD and check.

_i:_ sheep ____ rip ____ sweet ____ sip ____ steal ____ meal ____ bin

____ bean ____ six ____ knit ____ chip ____ lit ____ kneel

Stress for Clarity

One part of an English word may be stressed more than others. The words below are stressed on the first syllable. Listen to the CD and repeat the words as you hear them.

BASEball	MUsic	FLOWer	TEAcher	PLAYer	COffee
MOUNtain	RIVer	STUdent	LANguage	TAxi	SEAson
DICtionary	SCIentist	NEWSpaper	MAgazine	ENvelope	REStaurant

Grammar Review: Present Progressive Verb Form

Form: *am, is,* or *are* + present participle (verb *-ing*)

Use: To show action that began in the past, continues now, and will continue into the future.

I am reading now.
She is studying now.
They are shaking hands now.

Write the progressive form of each verb.

simple	present participle	simple	present participle
keep	*keeping*	change	______
take	*taking*	see	______
sleep	______	write	______
make	______	hold	______
eat	______	learn	______
do	______	practice	______
buy	______		

Fill in each blank with the correct form of the verb in parentheses.

1. Usually, I (walk) ______ to school. But now it (rain) ______, so I (ride) ______ the bus.
2. David and Julie (sit) ______ at the table. They (talk) ______ about the test.
3. Every day, Sam (cook) ______ his own dinner. But now he is sick, so I (cook) ______ it for him.
4. "Is John home?"
   "No, he (play) ______ baseball in the park now.
5. "What (do) ______ you ______?"
   "I (study) ______ English."

Compare your answers with a partner. Then listen to the CD and check. DL 15 CD 1-15

Unit 3

Someone You Should Know

Warm-Up

Look at these pictures of people. Use the words in the box to describe each person.

Describing People

blonde hair well-dressed young straight hair thin beard casually-dressed elderly

Speech Key 3.1

It's all in the details! Specific information will make your speech more interersting.

1. ________________ ________________
2. ________________ ________________
3. ________________ ________________
4. ________________ ________________

Now, practice describing your partner using these models. Talk about many details.

1. He/She is ________________.
2. He/She has ________________.

Maintaining Posture

When making a speech, you communicate with words and with your body. Your body can communicate confidence. But it can also distract your audience if you aren't careful.

Speech Key 3.2

Control your body! It can communicate confidence and make your speech more powerful.

Communicating Confidence

1. Keep your back straight. Don't slouch your shoulders.
2. Place your feet shoulder-width apart.
3. Face the audience. Don't turn your back to them.
4. Remain steady. Don't sway from side to side.
5. Control your hands. Don't shuffle papers or cover your face.

Troubleshooting

Look at these speakers. Each person is making a common error. Finish the sentences to identify the error and give advice.

1. He should not *sway*.
   He should *remain steady*.

3. He should not ________________.
   He should ________________.

2. She should not ________________.
   She should ________________.

4. She should not ________________.
   She should ________________.

Building Your Speech: Descriptive Details

We can describe people in different ways: What do they look like? What are their personalities like? What do they do?

APPEARANCE
- He is very tall, about 185 cm.
- He has short, dark hair.
- He is always well-dressed. He wears a suit and tie every day.
- He is very athletic. He goes to the gym every day and lifts weights.

INTERESTS
- He likes to watch baseball on TV. His favorite team is the Chicago Cubs.
- He enjoys playing chess.
- Every Sunday he plays with his two sons.

My brother, Bryan

HIS JOB
- He works for IBM. He is a salesman. He sells computer networks to companies around the world.

PERSONALITY
- He has a great sense of humor.
- He always smiles.
- He is very intelligent. He got all A's in college.
- He is very polite. He always holds the door for other people.

ABILITIES
- He can speak Spanish fluently. He uses it every day for work.
- He knows how to fly an airplane!
- He got his pilot's license recently.

My brother, Bryan, is someone you should know because he always helps a friend.

Now listen to the CD. The speaker will describe her brother, Bryan. Try to follow the different ways Bryan is described. What other details do you hear?

Practice

Work with a partner. Take the details from the box and write them under the correct headings to describe the famous person below. Then, try to guess his name.

Descriptive Details	He is very competitive.	He won six championships.
	He never boasts about his talent.	He is very humble.
	He is almost 2 meters tall.	He can also act.
	He tries to win every game he plays.	He is very tall.
	He enjoys playing golf in his retirement.	He played for the Chicago Bulls.
	He is African-American.	He can jump very high.
	He was in a movie called "Space Jam."	He played in the NBA.
	He can slam-dunk a basketball.	He shaves his head.
	He plays in charity golf tournaments.	

APPEARANCE

- *He is very tall.*
  - *He is almost 2 meters tall.*
- ______
- ______

PERSONALITY

- ______
  - ______
- ______
  - ______

INTERESTS

- ______
  - ______

HIS JOB

- ______
  - ______
  - ______

ABILITIES

- ______
  - ______
- *He can also act.*
  - ______

______ is someone you should know because he is the best at what he does.

Now listen to the CD and check your answers. DL 17 CD 1-17

Prepare

Now think about someone you admire. It can be a famous person, or someone you know personally. Write a short (2–3 minutes) speech to introduce this person to your classmates.

Someone You Should Know

____

Practice

Now practice your speech with a partner. Take notes on your partner's performance, for both content and delivery.

Speech Content

general points	specific details
______	______
______	______
______	______
______	______
______	______
______	______

What else would you like to know? ________________

Speech Delivery

	good	needs work
Eye Contact	____	____
Feet Shoulder-width Apart	____	____
Back Straight	____	____
Facing Audience	____	____
Busy Hands	____	____

Perform

Perform your speech for your group or your class. Practice making eye contact and controlling your body language.

Evaluation

As your classmates make their speeches, follow the example and fill in the evaluation chart. Make note of mistakes in body language.

Name	Swaying	Busy Hands	Back Not Straight	Back to Audience	Comments
Sayaka Kondo	*///*	*//*	*/*	*///*	*Sometimes touches her nose. Also turns to the board too often.*

Sound Pronunciation

Let's practice long "æ" and short "e" sounds.

[e] This is a short vowel sound.
▶ pen, hen, when, friend, spend

[æ] This is a long vowel sound.
▶ cat, hat, fat, apple, stack

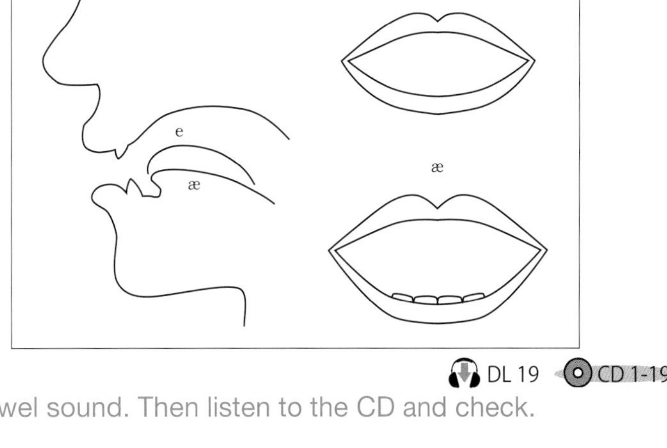

Now, listen to the CD DL 18 CD 1-18 and repeat.

DL 19 CD 1-19

Write "e" or "æ" on the line to describe the vowel sound. Then listen to the CD and check.

_e_ end ____ can ____ plan ____ sandwich ____ said ____ fed ____ bread ____ axe

____ bend ____ hand ____ fad ____ wed ____ black ____ family ____ intend ____ band

Stress for Clarity

The modals *can* and *can't* have different pronunciation depending on their position in a sentence. Listen to the CD and repeat. DL 20 CD 1-20

1. I can speak three languages.
2. Yes, I really can.
3. I can't speak Chinese.
4. I want to go, but I can't.

Pronouncing *Can* and *Can't*

When *can* comes at the beginning or in the middle of a statement, the vowel is silent.
When *can* comes at the end of a statement, it is articulated with the long *a* vowel sound.
When *can't* comes at the beginning or in the middle of a statement, the *t* is silent and can hardly be heard at all.
When *can't* comes at the end of a statement, the *t* is clearly heard.

Grammar Review: Modals for Advice and Ability

Form: *should, ought to, had better,* or *can* + simple verb

Use: *Should, ought to,* and *had better* are used to offer advice and can be either positive or negative. *Can* is used to express ability.

Careful! The main verb does not change:
X He can plays the guitar.
O He can play the guitar.

Examples

1. You should see Tokyo Tower when you go to Tokyo.
2. Should I carry an umbrella today?
3. He shouldn't smoke so much. It's not healthy.
4. We had better study for the test.
5. They had better not travel without insurance.
6. I can play the guitar, but I can't play the piano.
7. Can you speak any other languages?

*Notice that the modal comes before the subject in a question.
**Ought to* is usually used only in the positive.

Give advice in response to the first sentence. Use *should* or *should not* with one of the expressions in the box.

take a vacation	see a doctor	stay up so late
exercise more	check the dictionary	
walk alone at night	eat fast food	ask the teacher

1. A: I don't understand this word.
   B: You should check the dictionary.
2. A: I have a fever and a sore throat.
   B: ______________________
3. A: This neighborhood is dangerous.
   B: ______________________
4. A: I want to lose weight.
   B: ______________________
5. A: I want to be more muscular.
   B: ______________________
6. A: I can't wake up for my 9 a.m. class.
   B: ______________________
7. A: I don't understand this grammar point.
   B: ______________________
8. A: I haven't had a day off in over a year.
   B: ______________________

DL 21 CD 1-21

Compare with a partner. Then, listen to the CD. Check your answers.

Unit 4

Have You Ever Been There?

Warm-Up

Look at these pictures of famous cities. Make a list of things to do and places to see for each city.

Things to Do and Places to See

see the Statue of Liberty   go shopping in Ginza   go to a Yankees game
try great Japanese food   visit Big Ben   tour Buckingham Palace   ride a double-decker bus
see a Broadway show   walk around the Imperial Palace

1. ______________________
____
____
* ______________________

2. ______________________
____
____
* ______________________

3. ______________________
____
____
* ______________________

* Add your own idea. Compare with a partner.

Now, ask your partner about the places and activities.

Example: Have you ever ridden a double-decker bus?
Yes, I have.
No, I haven't.

Speech Key 4.1

Ask your audience questions. This helps create a warm relationship.

Body Language: Using Gestures

We communicate with both our words and our hands. By using gestures effectively, you can make your speech more interesting and easier to understand.

Speech Key 4.2

Use gestures naturally to make your speech more interesting and easier to understand.

Key Points about Gestures

1. Emphasize key points with clear, simple gestures.
2. Gestures guide the audience by adding visual reinforcement.
3. Gestures should be spontaneous. If you plan gestures, they may seem unnatural.
4. Don't overdo it! If your hands are too busy, your gestures will become a distraction. Rest your hands at your sides from time to time.

Practice

Listen to the CD. Match the number of the speech excerpt to the correct gesture. DL 22 CD 1-22

Speech Key 4.3

By learning and practicing many gestures, you are more likely to use them naturally in your speech.

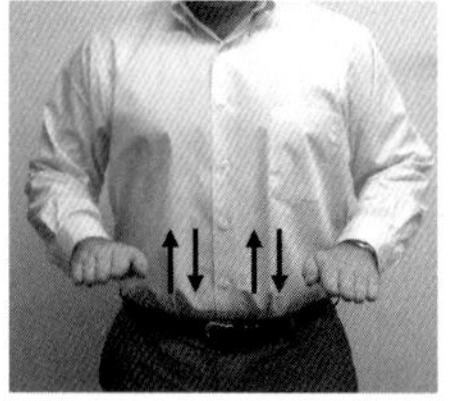

1. ____

2. ____

3. ____

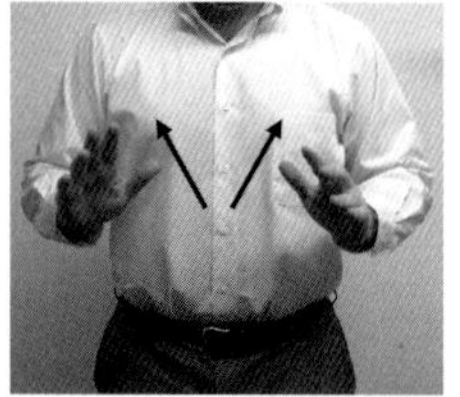

4. ____

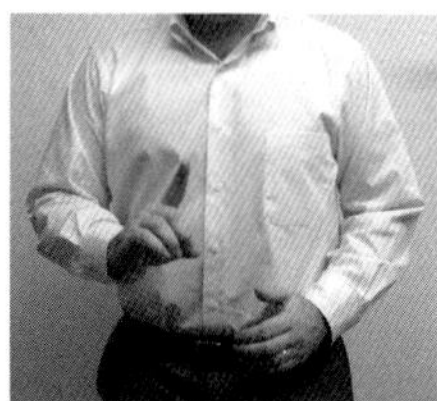

5. ____

Now compare your answers with a partner. Listen again and check.

Practice

For each statement, think of a gesture to emphasize the point. Then work with a partner and practice making the gesture.

1. Interest rates have been falling recently.
2. I promise, this is the truth.
3. No one knows what really happened.
4. Please be quiet.
5. We had to stop the project.
6. I had to repeat it over and over again.
7. They did a great job!
8. I have two brothers and one sister.
9. Tokyo is larger than New York.
10. I was very nervous.
11. Never try this at home.

My first point is…

Now perform your gestures for the class. Let them try to guess which point you are trying to emphasize.

Practice

Listen to the CD. Work with a partner and think of a gesture for each excerpt.  DL 23  CD 1-23

Building Your Speech: Brainstorming & Clustering

Brainstorming means "to generate ideas." Simply by listing words and details related to your purpose, you can find something to say. Clustering is a method of generating and organizing a lot of details very quickly. Even if you don't use all of the details in your speech, it is an effective way to get started when you have difficulty thinking of what to say.

Clustering

1. Think of your subject. Write it in the middle of the page and draw a square around it.
2. Think of as many topics related to your subject as you can. Write the topics down in the squares around the subjects, as in the example.
3. Think of as many details or points about each topic as can. Write them below each topic in the squares.

Brainstorming
US cities I know:
New York
✓ Fort Collins
Chicago
Atlanta
Champaign

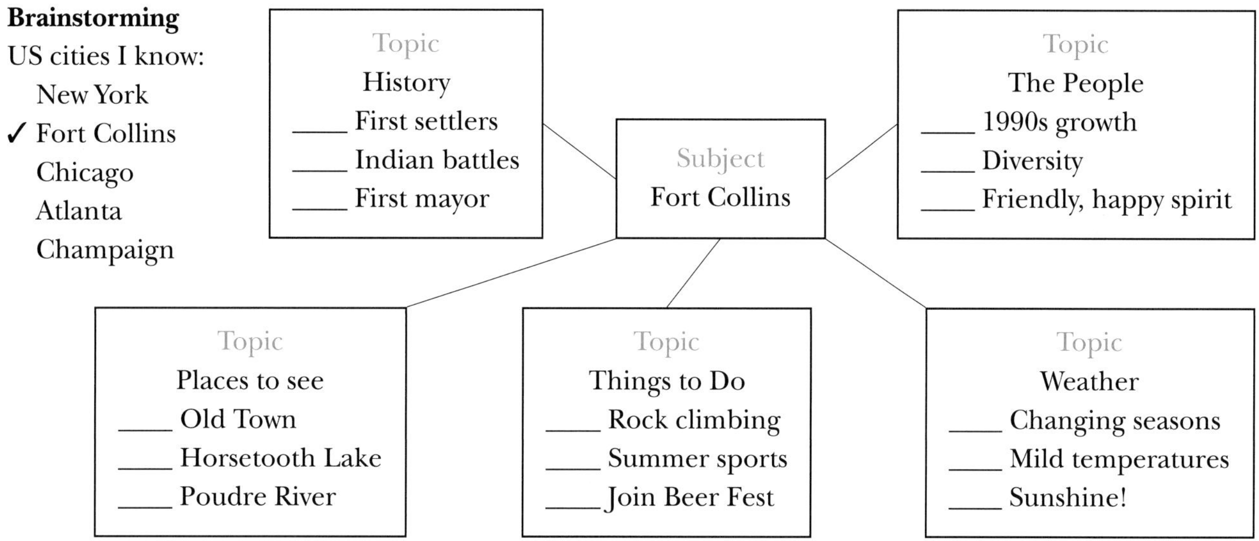

Now listen to the CD. Put a check (✓) next to the details you hear about Fort Collins.

online video DL 24 CD 1-24

Practice

First, brainstorm a list of interesting places you've been to. Then, try clustering to generate details.

Brainstorming
Interesting places I've been to:

____

____

____

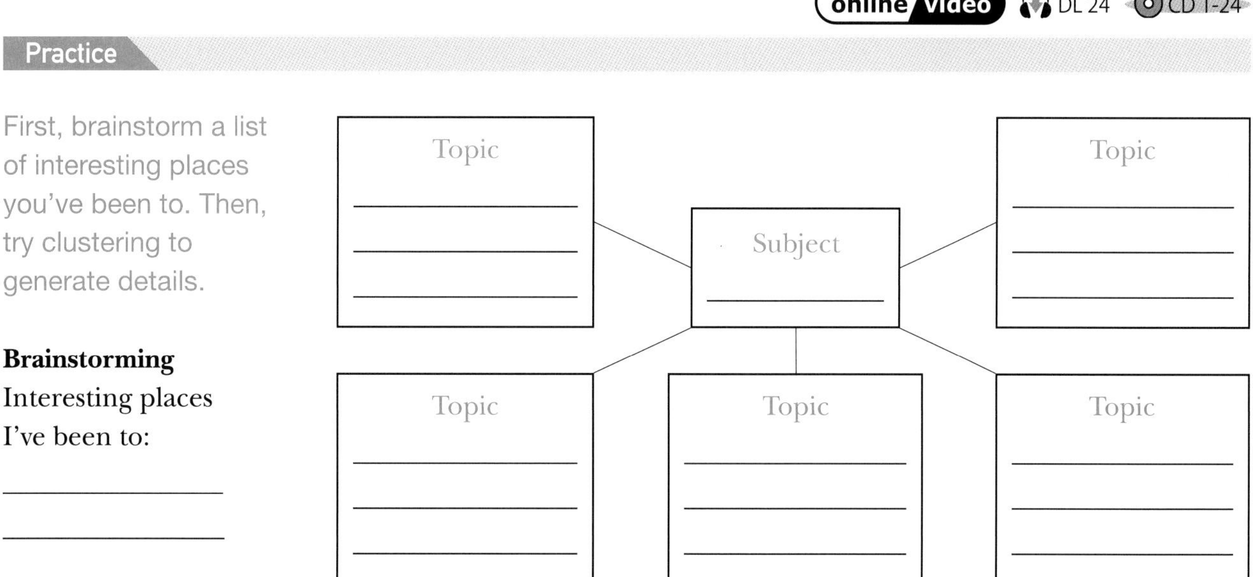

Prepare

Now take the information from the clustering activity and outline a short (3–4 minute) speech about an interesting place you've been to.

Have You Ever Been There?

____

____

____

____

____

____

____

____

____

____

____

____

____

Practice

Work with a partner and practice your speech. Help your partner identify strengths and weaknesses in both content and use of gestures.

Speech Content

What is most interesting about the speech? ____________

____

____

How can this speech be improved? ____________

____

____

What else would you like to know? ____________

____

____

Speech Delivery: Gestures

	good	needs work
Spontaneous	_____	_____
Appropriate	_____	_____
Natural	_____	_____
Too many	_____	_____

Perform

Now perform your speech for your class or group. While your classmates are performing, note how many gestures they use. Discuss them afterward.

Sound Pronunciation

Let's practice the short "ʌ" and long "ɑ:" sounds.

[ʌ] This is a short vowel sound.
 luck, stuck, cup, bug, cut

[ɑ:] This is a long vowel sound.
 car, heart, start, cart, March

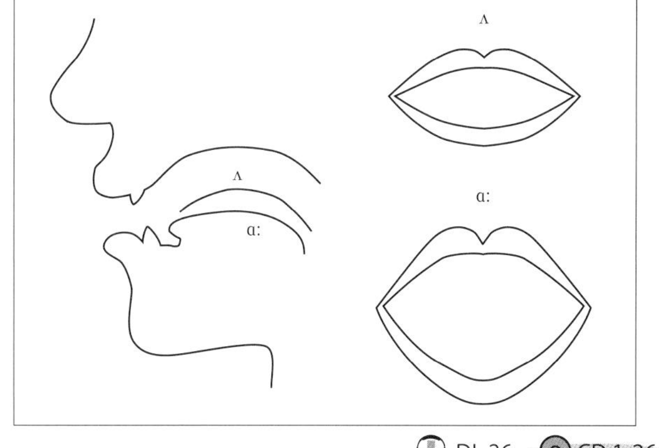

Now, listen to the CD DL 25 CD 1-25 and repeat.

DL 26 CD 1-26

Write "ʌ" or "ɑ:" on the line to describe the vowel sound. Then listen to the CD and check.

_ʌ_ what ____ park ____ chart ____ but ____ cluck ____ art ____ mart ____ muck

____ hard ____ part ____ barn ____ much ____ bun ____ dart ____ hut ____ shut

Stress for Meaning

Listen to the CD. Underline the word that is stressed in each sentence. DL 27 CD 1-27
Then circle the choice that best describes the meaning of that stress.

1. I bought three cigars.
   a. not two?
   b. not cigarettes?
   c. did not borrow?

2. I think Bob has the best voice.
   a. not sure?
   b. not Steve?
   c. not second best?

3. Why don't you buy the red tie?
   a. not me?
   b. not the blue tie?
   c. not the red shirt?

Grammar Review: Present Perfect Verb Form

Form: *have/has* + past participle
In many cases the past and past participle of a verb are the same. In some cases the participle changes form. Memorize these important verbs.

Use: To talk about an indefinite time in the past. Used with *for* and *since* to talk about activity that began in the past and continues in the present.

Past Participles

simple	past	participle
take	took	*taken*
fly	flew	*flown*
begin	began	______________
go	went	______________
do	did	______________
see	saw	______________
know	knew	______________
choose	chose	______________
eat	ate	______________
drink	drank	______________

Examples

I have been to Paris many times.
My sister has toured Europe.
I have studied English for three years.
I have never seen the Yankees play.
Have you ever tried sushi?
I have lived in Tokyo since 2002.
Bob has passed the test.
Bob passed the test last month.*

*Notice that "last month" makes the time definite, so the simple past is used.

Listen to the CD and repeat. DL 28 CD 1-28

Use the verbs in the box to complete the sentences.
Use either the present perfect or the simple past form.

take	do	teach	drive	try	swim	drink	go	visit	know

1. I *have tried* sushi before, but not tempura.
2. I ____________________ my grandmother's house during summer vacation.
3. Jenny ____________________ photographs of many famous people.
4. Bob ____________________ sake many times.
5. Ken and Steve ____________________ in the ocean when they were children.
6. Sarah ____________________ her homework, so now she can watch TV.
7. John ____________________ to Australia last year.
8. Jim and Karen ____________________ each other for many years.
9. My brother ____________________ math at a high school since 1995.
10. I ____________________ a car only once before.

Compare your answers with a partner. Then listen to the CD and check. DL 29 CD 1-29

Unit 5

How to Make a Spectacular Dish!

Warm-Up

Look at the pictures of four different dishes. Can you name each dish and its ingredients?

	1.	2.	3.	4.
What's it called?	*burrito*			
What's in it?			*katsuobushi*	

okonomiyaki pad thai burrito tortilla tomato sauce lasagna peanut oil cabbage salsa cheese rice noodles katsuobushi

Using Your Voice I: Enunciating

In formal presentation, it is important to enunciate each syllable loudly and clearly.

DL 30 CD 1-30

Listen to the CD. You will hear the following statements twice. Which is enunciated better? Put a check (✓) next to A or B.

1. I have been working in Toronto for about a year. A ____ B ____
2. I'm thinking of buying a bottle of beer. A ____ B ____

Speech Key 5.1

Clear enunciation makes your speech easier to understand.

Enunciating Clearly

1. Check a new word's pronunciation in the dictionary. Check the syllables and vowels.
2. Practice in the mirror. Notice how your mouth, tongue, lips, and jaw all move. Exaggerate the movements until enunciation becomes natural.
3. Slow down! Speaking too quickly makes it difficult to enunciate.
4. Warm up. Use tongue-twisters to practice enunciation.

Enunciation Practice: Tongue Twisters

Practice saying these tongue-twisters with a partner. Make sure to enunciate each word fully. Check your partner's enunciation.

1. She sells sea shells by the sea shore.
2. Six thick thistle sticks. Six thick thistles stick.
3. Three free throws.
4. Crisp crusts crackle crunchily.
5. Freshly fried fresh fish flesh.

Now listen to the CD. During the pauses, repeat the sentences.  

Building Your Speech: Using Transitions & Connecting Words

Transitions are short phrases that connect the parts of your presentation. They guide the audience as you move from point to point. We can use different transitions for different purposes:

> **Speech Key 5.2**
> Transitions guide your audience as you move from point to point.

To announce the start of a new topic	To list items in sequence	To announce examples	To restate a key point	To conclude
First, I'd like to…	First… Second… Third…	For example… For instance…	In other words…	In conclusion…
Next, I'll explain…	First… Next… After that… Finally…	Let me illustrate with an example…	To put it another way…	To recap…
Now, let's turn to…	One… Another… Yet another…	An example will help illustrate…	In short…	To sum up…
Finally, let's look at…		Here's an example…	Let me stress again…	In summary…

We can also use connecting words to show the relationship between ideas in a sentence:

To show a cause	To show a result	To show a contrast	To show an addition
because	so	but	and
since	therefore	however	in addition
because of	as a result	nevertheless	also
due to	consequently	yet	moreover

Listen to the CD and repeat the words and phrases during the pauses.  CD 1-32

Practice

Read this recipe for Mike's famous breakfast burrito. Fill in the blanks with transitions and connecting words from page 26.

Ingredients

4 tortillas 4 large eggs 1 tomato (diced) 200 g Mexican sausage
1 potato (diced) 100 g cheddar cheese 100 ml hot salsa

Today I'd like to tell you how to make a spectacular dish—a breakfast burrito. Before you begin, you'll have to go shopping. You will need all of the ingredients you see listed. There are many items, _________ they are not expensive, _______________ it's really simple to make. _______________, cook the sausage in a skillet. _______________, add the potatoes and cook until they are brown. _______________, drain the fat. Warm the tortillas over the fire. _______________, they burn easily, _______________ be careful! Then, scramble the eggs with the potatoes and sausage. When the eggs are done, divide the skillet contents among the four tortillas. _______________, add the cheese and tomatoes. _______________, roll the tortilla. _______________, pour the salsa over the top. And there you have it! Enjoy!

Compare your answers with a partner. Then listen to the CD and check. DL 33 CD 1-33

Practice

Now the speaker will explain the steps in repairing a flat tire on a bicycle. Number the steps from 1 to 10.

____ Pump air into the tire.
____ Find the hole in the inner tube.
____ Remove the wheel.
____ Put the wheel back on the bike.
__1__ Let the air out of the tire.
____ Put the tire back on the rim.
____ Take the inner tube out of the tire.
____ Remove the tire from the rim.
____ Patch the hole in the inner tube.
____ Put the inner tube back on the tire.

Compare your answers with a partner. Then listen to the CD. online video DL 34 CD 1-34
Notice the transitions and connecting words.

Brainstorming

Brainstorm a list of possible speech topics. Think of things you know how to do or make. Think about what your audience (your classmates) might be interested in learning to do or make.

Things I Can Do	Things I Can Make
Fix a flat tire	*Breakfast Burrito*

Prepare

Now choose one of the topics from your brainstorming list. On a separate sheet of paper, write a short speech. Remember to include transitions to guide your audience.

Practice

Practice performing your speech with a partner. Check your partner's enunciation and use of transitions.

Notes on Enunciation

Problem words: ______________________________

____

____

____

____

Notes on Transitions

Which transitions are used? ______________________

____

Are they used appropriately? ____ yes ____ no

What connecting words are used? ______________

____

Are they used appropriately? ____ yes ____ no

Suggestions for improvement ______________

____

Performance & Evaluation

Perform your speech for your class or group. As your classmates make their speeches, follow the example and evaluate their enunciation and use of transitions.

Name	Use of transitions	Use of connecting words	Problems with enunciation	Comments
Yuko Kanda	///	///	//	*Transitions good; practice enunciation of "firstly" and "finally."*

Sound Pronunciation

Let's practice short "u" and long "u:" vowel sounds.

[u] This is a short vowel sound.
▸ look, put, shook, hook, book, took

[u:] This is a long vowel sound.
▸ shoot, fool, pool, stool, rule, mule

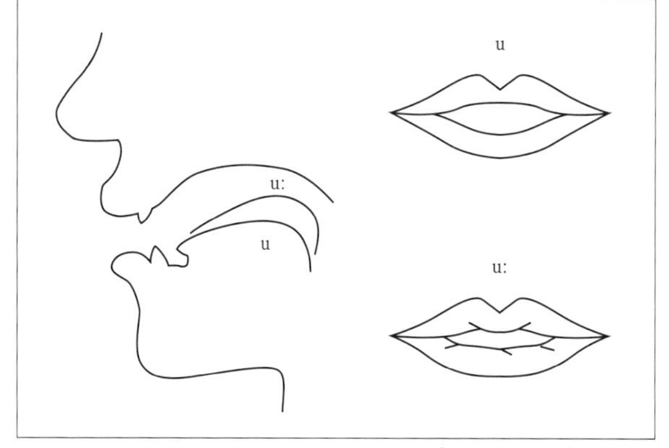

Now, listen to the CD DL 35 CD 1-35 and repeat.

DL 36 CD 1-36

Write "u" or "u:" on the line to describe the vowel sound. Then listen to the CD and check.

_u:_ route ____ crook ____ stool ____ cool ____ brook ____ could ____ wool
____ good ____ jewel ____ cruel ____ should ____ pool ____ drool

Practice

DL 37 CD 1-37

One of the most common enunciation errors is the dropping of the final *g* sound in progressive verb forms and participial adjectives. Listen to the CD and repeat during the pauses. Make sure to enunciate the final *g* fully.

working, living, winning, running, happening, going, wishing, finding, studying, making, writing, feeling, sleeping, treating, exciting, interesting, boring, amazing, compelling, inviting, amusing

Vocabulary Builder: Strong Adjectives

Strong adjectives can make your presentation more dramatic and interesting. Use the clues on the right to complete the puzzle. Work with a partner or in a small group. Use a dictionary, if necessary.

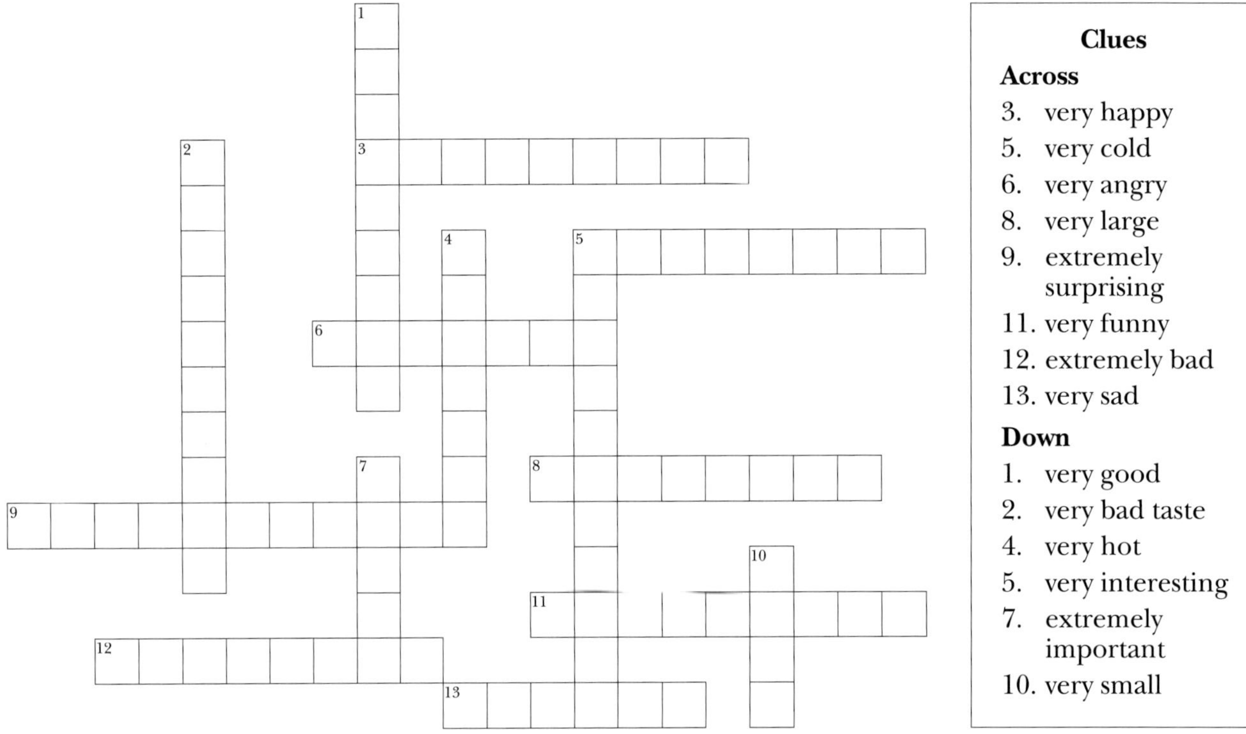

Clues
Across
3. very happy
5. very cold
6. very angry
8. very large
9. extremely surprising
11. very funny
12. extremely bad
13. very sad
Down
1. very good
2. very bad taste
4. very hot
5. very interesting
7. extremely important
10. very small

Now listen to the CD. Repeat the strong adjectives during the pauses. DL 38 CD 1-38

Practice

Rewrite the following sentences using strong adjectives.

1. It is absolutely cold in Chicago in January.

   ____

2. That movie was very bad. I've never seen a worse movie.

   ____

3. We were very scared. We almost died!

   ____

4. I think it would be very interesting to live abroad.

   ____

5. That food tastes very bad. I thought I would die when I ate it.

   ____

Practice your sentences out loud. Place extra stress on the strong adjectives for emphasis.

Unit 6

Let Me Tell You What Happened...

Warm-Up

Look at this list of important events in a person's life. Put a (✓) check next to events that have already happened in your life. Put a question mark (?) next to events that may happen in your life in the future.

____ First day of kindergarten	____ Getting a driver's license	____ First day of work
____ Graduation from high school	____ Birth of a child	____ First apartment
____ Wedding day	____ Graduation from college	

Now write the name of the event under the correct picture. Discuss these events with a partner. Which ones do you remember? What was memorable about the event?

1. ____________ 2. ____________ 3. ____________ 4. ____________ 5. ____________

Using Your Voice II: Projecting

The most interesting speech will go unnoticed if no one can hear you. You'll need to project your voice to ensure that everyone can hear you loudly and clearly.

Using Your Diaphragm

Place your hand on your stomach and say "HA" loudly. Do you feel that muscle move? That is your diaphragm. It is pushing air up from your lungs to project your voice. When you breathe from your diaphragm, your stomach moves but your chest doesn't. By learning how to breathe through your diaphragm, you can make your voice richer, clearer, and louder.

Projecting Your Voice

1. Don't shout or scream! This will only annoy your audience and hurt your throat.
2. Remember to breathe deeply using your diaphragm. The power of your voice comes from the movement of air over the vocal chords.
3. Never turn your back to the audience.
4. Drink only water before a speech. Sweet drinks or milk can dampen your voice.

Speech Key 6.1

Projecting your voice communicates confidence and gets everyone's attention.

Exercise your diaphragm. Follow these steps to practice breathing with your diaphragm:

1. When practicing your speech, lie on the floor and begin talking. You'll notice how much stronger your voice is. That's because you are using only your diaphragm.
2. Stand up, take a deep breath in through your nose for five seconds.
3. Hold your breath for two seconds.
4. Breathe out slowly through your mouth.
5. Repeat.
6. Continue practicing your speech, breathing in through your nose and breathing out through your diaphragm as you speak.

Building Your Speech: Explaining Events

When we explain events that happened in the past, we must give our audience enough information to understand what happened. To do this, generate details by brainstorming *Wh~* questions.

- Who are the people involved in the event? Describe them. How did they become involved? Why are they important?
- What happened? Brainstorm as many details as possible about the event. What did you do? What did other people do? What was most memorable? Was anything surprising? What was the mood? How did you feel?
- Where did the event happen? Describe the place. Did it happen in more than one place? What are the important details about the place?
- When did it happen? Was it long ago or recently? How old were you at the time? How is the time important?
- Why did it happen? Why was this event important? How did it effect you? Did it cause a change in your life? What was the result?

Practice

Listen to the CD. You will hear about an event from the speaker's past. Listen and write down as many details as you can for each *Wh~* question.

online video

DL 39 CD 1-39

Who?	What?	Where?	When?	Why?
______	______	______	______	______
______	______	______	______	______
______	______	______	______	______
______	______	______	______	______

Check with a partner. Then listen again and check your answers. Also, write down any strong adjectives you hear.

Strong Adjectives

____

____

____

____

Group Work: Audience Analysis

In both conversation and formal speech, think about the needs of your audience. Who are they? What do they know? What do they need to know? How do I want them to respond to me? This simple but fun exercise can show you how we communicate with different audiences in a different way. Read the situation in the box. Each group must write a letter to explain the accident to a different audience.

Group 1: Write a letter to your friend, whose car you destroyed.
Group 2: Write a letter to your parents, who will help you pay for the damage.
Group 3: Write a letter to the owner of the convenience store that you damaged.
Group 4: Write a letter to the police, who will fill out a report about the accident.

Situation

You borrowed your friend's car for a few hours and decided to go play pachinko. On the way to the pachinko parlour, you had an accident, crashing the car into a convenience store. It was your fault. No one was hurt, but the car is destroyed.

When you are finished, read your letter to the class. How are the letters different? How are they the same?

Brainstorming

First, work with a partner and brainstorm a list of important past events in your life that might be interesting to your classmates. Now, choose one topic from your list and brainstorm as many *Wh~* details as you can.

Interesting Events in My Life

traveling abroad last year.

Who?	What?	Where?	When?	Why?

Prepare

Now prepare your speech on a separate sheet of paper. As you prepare, think about your audience (in this case, your classmates and teacher). Who are they? What do they know about you? What do they need to know to understand the event? Try to use some of the transitions you learned in Unit 5. Also, try to use some strong adjectives to make your speech more exciting!

Practice

Now work with a partner and practice your speech. Check for voice projection. Also, make a list of the *Wh~* details you hear. Make suggestions for improvement.

Notes on Enunciation & Projection

Problem words: ______________________

____

____

____

Comments on projection: ______________________

____

____

____

Notes on Details

Who? ______________________

What? ______________________

Where? ______________________

When? ______________________

Why? ______________________

What else do you want to know? ______________________

____

____

Perform

Perform your speech for your group or class. Remember to project your voice.

Evaluation

As others are giving their presentations, follow the example and evaluate their performances. Pay particular attention to enunciation, projection, and details and rate performance on a scale of 1 (poor) to 10 (good).

Name	Projection	Enunciation	Details	Comments
Mitsunori Itoh	*8*	*6*	*9*	*Great details, strong voice. Some words I couldn't hear fully.*

Sound Pronunciation

Let's practice short "ɑ" and long "ɔ:".

[ɑ] This is a short vowel sound.
▸ shock, knock, top, hot, shot, watt

[ɔ:] This is a long vowel sound.
▸ fall, wall, caught, water, all, walk

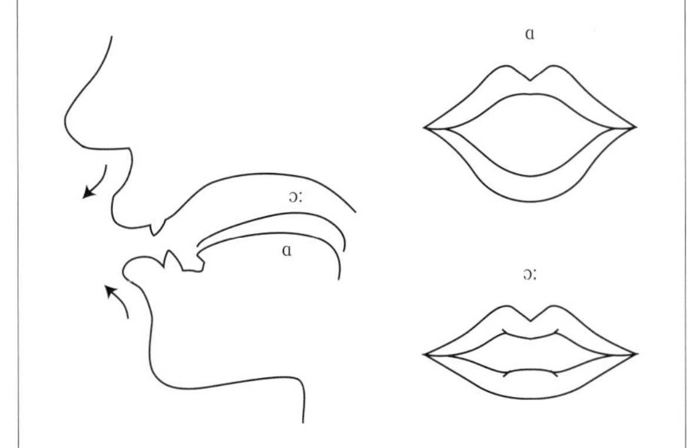

Now, listen to the CD DL 40 CD 1-40 and repeat.

DL 41 CD 1-41

Write "ɑ" or "ɔ:" on the line to describe the vowel sound. Then listen to the CD and check.

_ɔ:_ mall ____ not ____ cot ____ stall ____ crawl ____ clock ____ drawl

____ pot ____ maul ____ box ____ shawl ____ sock ____ mock

Intonation Practice: Listing

Your voice usually rises at the end of a question.
Would you like a cup of coffee?

However, when you list choices in a question, your voice falls on the last item.
Would you like coffee, tea, or milk?

The same is true of listed items in statements.
Every morning I wake up, eat breakfast, brush my teeth, and go to work.

Listen to the CD and repeat. Then, write three statements or questions containing lists. Practice saying the sentences with correct intonation. Work with a partner. DL 42 CD 1-42

Grammar Review: Past Progressive

Form: *was/were* + verb + *ing*

Use: To show an event in progress in the past, or to show the relationship between two events or times in the past.

At 9:00pm last night…
I was watching TV.
Carol was sleeping.
Bob was doing his homework.
Jane and Ted were listening to music.
My cat and I were sitting on the sofa.

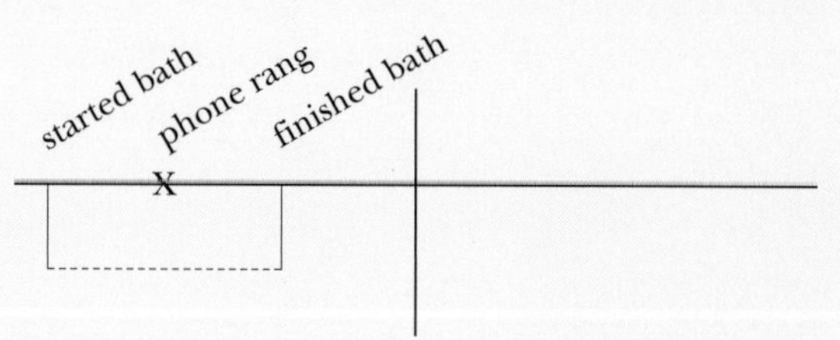

While I was taking a bath, the phone rang.
I was taking a bath when the phone rang.

Notes: *While* is used with the progressive verb, but *when* is used with the simple past. When the sentence begins with a time clause, use a comma before the main clause.

Combine these sentences using *while* or *when*.

1. The baseball game ended. I was getting a hot dog.

   ____

2. We were walking to the train station. We met Bill.

   ____

3. It started to rain. They were walking home.

   ____

Fill in each blank with the correct form of the verb in parentheses.

1. While I (watch) ______________ TV, someone (knock) ______________ on the door.
2. The teacher (give) ______________ a test when the students (arrive) ______________.

Compare your answers with a partner. Then listen to the CD and check.  DL 43  CD 1-43

Unit 7

In the World Today...

Warm-Up

What's in the news recently? Make a list of interesting current events for each category. Work with a partner.

Sports	Politics	Crime	Entertainment
__________	__________	__________	__________
__________	__________	__________	__________
__________	__________	__________	__________

Which events are international? Which ones are national? Which ones are local?
Which events are important? Why? Which events are the most interesting to you? Why?

Using Your Voice III: Pacing Yourself

People tend to speak too quickly when they are nervous. This is one of the most common problems speakers face. If you speak too quickly, your audience may not be able to understand you. If you speak too slowly, your audience may lose interest. Speaking at a comfortable, natural pace is a key to success.

> **Speech Key 7.1**
>
> By speaking at a comfortable, natural pace, you help your audience maintain interest and understanding.

How to Control Your Pace

1. Focus on enunciation. This will help you slow down.
2. Practice phrasing. Just as in writing, there are pauses and breaks in your speech.
3. Stop and take a breath from time to time. Take a drink of water. Give your audience time to comprehend your ideas.
4. Watch your audience for clues that your pace is off.

How to Check Your Pace

Is your audience falling asleep? Do their eyes look glazed? Your pace is too slow!
Is your audience taking notes very quickly? Do they look confused? Your pace is too fast!
Are people nodding their heads, smiling, watching you carefully? Your pace is probably just right!

Practice

Listen to the CD. You will hear 6 speech excerpts. Put a check (✓) next to the ones with good pace. If the pace is too fast, write "F." If the pace is too slow, write "S." DL 44 CD 1-44

1. ____ 2. ____ 3. ____ 4. ____ 5. ____ 6. ____

Practice

Practice pacing by reading out loud. Look at this paragraph, written by Helen Keller. Check the pronunciation carefully and decide where there should be pauses. Then, practice reading out loud until you can say it naturally.

> Have you ever been at sea in a dense fog, when it seemed as if a tangible white darkness shut you in, and the great ship, tense and anxious, groped her way toward the shore with plummet and sounding-line, and you waited with beating heart for something to happen? I was like that ship before my education began, only I was without compass or sounding-line and had no way of knowing how near the harbor was. "Light, give me light!" was the wordless cry of my soul, and the light of love shone on me in that very hour.
>
> Helen Keller
>
> *The Day Language Came into My Life*

DL 45 

Now listen to the CD. Is your performance similar to the recording? How is it different?

Building Your Speech: Selecting Details

In Unit 6, we learned to generate details by asking *Wh~* questions. But you might not want to use all of the details. Use only the most interesting and relevant details.

Speech Key 7.2

Give your audience only the most interesting and relevant details.

A reporter has brainstormed details about an earthquake in Hokkaido. Put a check (✓) next to the most relevant details.

____ Most of the injuries were not serious.
____ There is no way to accurately predict quakes.
____ An earthquake hit Kobe in 1995.
____ Zushima is famous for its seafood.
____ The quake had a magnitude of 4.5.
____ The town of Zushima in Hokkaido was hardest hit.
____ The quake happened at 6:13 a.m.
____ Older homes suffered most of the damage.
____ 30 people were hurt, but no deaths were reported.
____ Japan has more earthquakes than America.
____ The epicenter was 200 km east of Hokkaido.
____ Firefighters put out several fires caused by the quake.

Compare your answers with a partner. Then listen to the CD and check.  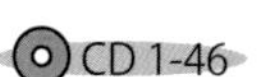

Building Your Speech II: Types of Statements

When our purpose is to explain an event, it is important to distinguish between facts and opinions. Facts are verifiable. We can do research to find out that they are true. An opinion is our judgment or feeling about the facts. People may have different opinions about the same event, but the facts do not change.

Fact: An earthquake hit Hokkaido at 6:13 a.m.
Opinion: The government should do more to help quake victims.

Read the following statements. Write "O" next to opinions, and an "F" next to facts.

____ Baseball is more exciting than soccer.
____ Japanese couples should have more children.
____ Japan has the 2nd largest economy in the world.
____ Math is difficult.
____ Teaching is a difficult job.
____ There are over 150 members in the U.N.
____ Teachers are paid less than lawyers.
____ English is an international language.
____ The birthrate in Japan is declining.
____ English should be a required subject.

Check your answers with a partner.
Then write two statements of fact and two statements of opinion.

Fact: ____
Fact: ____
Opinion: ____
Opinion: ____

Compare your answers with your group members.
Are your facts true? Do people agree with your opinions?

Practice

Listen to the CD. You will hear a presentation about a current event. First, identify the topic. Then in your own words, summarize the event, including only the most important details.

online video
DL 47 CD 1-47

Topic: ____
Summary: ____
____
____

What is the speaker's opinion about this event? What are his reasons? Write your answer below.

Opinion: ____
Reasons: 1. ____
2. ____
3. ____

Brainstorming

Look at your list of current events on page 37. Choose one that you would like to present to the class. Brainstorm as many details as you can about the event. Then think about your opinion of it.

When ____________________

____

Where ____________________

____

Who ____________________

____

What ____________________

____

Why ____________________

____

My opinion of the event:

I think that ____________________

____

because ____________________

____

Put a check (✓) next to the most relevant details. Explain your ideas to your group and see if they agree.

Prepare

Organize the most important details into a short (3–4 minute) presentation of the current event you've chosen. After you've explained the event, explain your opinion about it.

Current Event

Practice

Work with a partner and practice your presentation. Check your partner's pace and suggest improvements. Check the relevance of the details, too.

Notes on Pace

	yes	no
Too fast?	____	____
Too Slow?	____	____
Natural?	____	____

Suggestions for improvement:

____

____

Notes on Details

Most important details: ______________________________

____

Least important details: ______________________________

____

What do you want to know more about? __________________

____

What could be cut? ____________________________________

____

Perform

Perform your presentation for your group or the class.

Sound Pronunciation

Let's practice long "ə:r" and short "ə" vowel sounds.

[ə:r] This is a long vowel sound.
- stir, girl, hurl, swirl, turn, worm, earn

[ə] This is a very short vowel sound.
- photograph, camera, water, America, four o'clock, mother, about

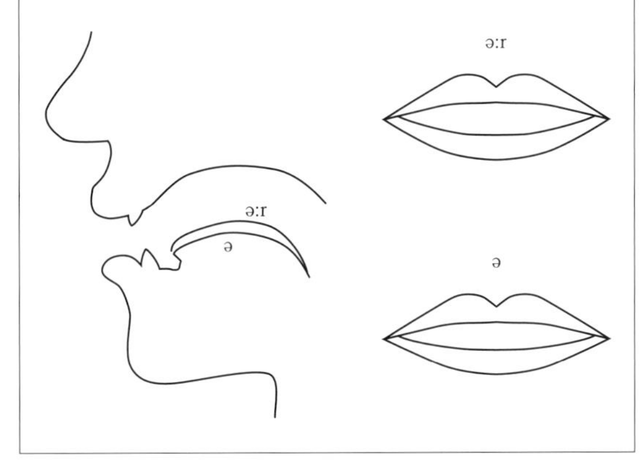

Now, listen to the CD and repeat. DL 48 CD 1-48

Underline the "ə" sound in each of the following words.

audience exaggerate promotion pronunciation appearance confidence

Now check your answers in your dictionary. Then listen to the CD and repeat. DL 49 CD 1-49

First, review "ɑ" and long "ɔ:" from Unit 6. Identify the vowel sound with "ɑ" "ɔ:" or "ə:r". Then listen to the CD and check. DL 50 CD 1-50

<u>ə:r</u> girl ____ not ____ haul ____ spot ____ smock ____ twirl ____ caught

____ rock ____ shirt ____ thought ____ dirt ____ dawn ____ stock

Stress for Clarity

In spoken English, the initial "h" is often silent, unless the word is emphasized with extra stress. Listen to the CD and repeat. DL 51 CD 1-51

Where did he park the car?
Who have you been talking to?
How did HE get here?
What's her favorite food?
How has he been lately?
You HAVE to see this movie!
How are his investments doing?
How long have you been waiting?

Grammar Review: Simple Connecting Words

Simple connecting words are used to show relationships between ideas. Using them makes your sentences more interesting and easier to understand.

Use *but* to show a contrast between ideas or opposites.
  I studied hard, but I failed the test.
  I love baseball, but I hate soccer.
Use *and* to show similarity between ideas, or a sequence.
  I studied hard, and I passed the test.
  I slept well, and I feel great!
Use *so* to show a result or consequence.
  English is an international language, so many people study it.
Use *because* to show a result or cause.
  I was late for class because I missed my train.
  Because I missed my train, I was late for class.

Fill in the blanks with the correct simple connector.

In New York today, there was a terrible accident, ____ fortunately no one was killed. A ferry boat carrying 35 passengers across the river crashed into a pier ____ the captain fell asleep on the job! Luckily, the boat was moving slowly, ____ the injuries were only minor bumps and bruises. The captain was fired, ____ the company apologized to the passengers. ____ of damage to the pier, ferry traffic was delayed for several hours. The police are still investigating the incident, ____ it is likely that the captain will be charged with a crime.

Listen to the CD and check your answers. DL 52 CD 1-52

Unit 8

Cause & Consequence

Warm-Up

Look at the problems on the left. Match them to their possible causes on the right. Work with a partner.

PROBLEMS	POSSIBLE CAUSES
global warming	lack of exercise, poor diet
obesity	reduced classroom hours
poor interpersonal skills	lack of support for families
youth violence	too much carbon dioxide in the air
NEETs	broken families, child abuse
declining birthrate	too much time using electronic media
declining academic achievement	poor job opportunities for young people

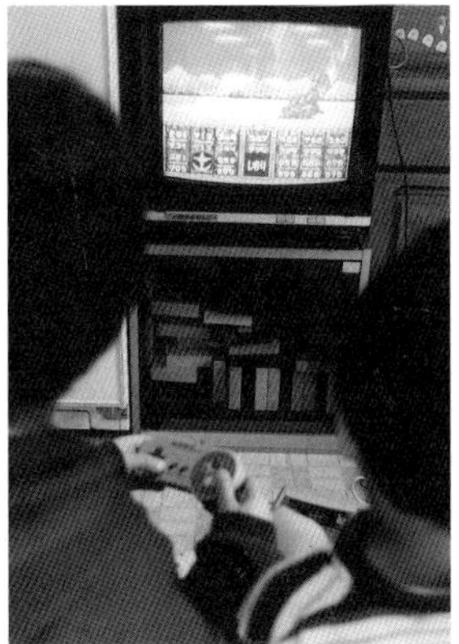

Now think of two more problems. They can be international, national, or local. What do you think might be the causes? Work with a partner.

PROBLEMS		POSSIBLE CAUSES
______________________	→	______________________
______________________	→	______________________

Using Your Voice IV: Expressing Yourself

When we speak, pace, pitch, volume, and stress can be varied to communicate a wide range of emotions, including excitement, urgency, seriousness, sympathy, and sadness. If you speak in a monotone voice, the audience will think you are not interested in your topic, and they will not be interested in it either.

How to Express Emotions

1. Think about the emotion you wish to convey.
2. Exaggerate normal pitch and rhythm.
3. Add stress on key words.
4. Raise your voice to get the attention of your audience.
5. Increase speed to generate suspense or excitement.
6. Combine stress with gestures.

Speech Key 8.1

Vary your pace, volume, pitch, and stress to communicate a wide range of emotions.

Listen to the CD. You will hear several statements read twice. Put a check (✓) next to "a" or "b" to indicate which is said with proper expression.

DL 53 CD 1-53

1. a ____ b ____
2. a ____ b ____
3. a ____ b ____
4. a ____ b ____
5. a ____ b ____
6. a ____ b ____
7. a ____ b ____
8. a ____ b ____
9. a ____ b ____
10. a ____ b ____

Practice

Listen to the CD. What emotion is being conveyed in each statement? DL 54 CD 1-54
Write the appropriate statement number next to each word.

____ excitement ____ worry ____ urgency ____ happiness ____ relief
____ surprise ____ anger ____ sympathy ____ sadness ____ seriousness

Compare your answers with a partner. Then listen again and check.

Practice

Read the following statements and decide what emotion should be conveyed. Then practice reading/saying each statement with a partner.

1. I never expected to be so lucky. ______________
2. On my wedding day, my wife was absolutely beautiful. ______________
3. I studied all night, but I still failed the test. ______________
4. I was furious when my father took the car keys away. ______________
5. David's mother died when he was a young boy. ______________

DL 55 CD 1-55
Now listen to the CD. Is your version similar? How is it different?

Now, write your own sentences for the following emotions. Practice saying them with a partner.

Worry: ____

Urgency: ____

Building Your Speech: Explaining Causes

Explaining the causes of problems or phenomena is a common purpose for many speakers. Success depends on how clearly and completely causes are explained.

Speech Key 8.2
Explaining complex causal relationships is an important skill in many fields.

The two statements below describe possible annual sales results for a company.
1. "Sales were much better than expected."
2. "We failed to meet our sales projections."

Read the six statements below. Each is a possible cause of one of the results above. Write a "1" next to the statements that are possible causes of the first result. Write a "2" next to the statements that are possible causes of the second result. Put a check (✓) next to the most important cause of each result.

DL 56 CD 1-56
Check your answers with a partner. Then listen to the CD. Notice the different tone of each speaker.

____ The economy is poor, and people have less money to buy our products.
____ Our sales team tried an aggressive new approach.
____ A new advertising campaign is giving our products more exposure.
____ Our main market competitor has reduced its prices.
____ We were able to lower our prices, making our products a better bargain.
____ Our competitor's products are faster and more efficient than ours.

Practice

Listen to the CD. You will hear a short presentation about the possible causes of gun violence in the United States. Put a check (✓) next to the possible causes you hear.

Possible Causes

1. ____ Americans are violent by nature.
2. ____ The US has few gun control laws.
3. ____ People are afraid.
4. ____ The news media makes people afraid.
5. ____ The US has a violent history.
6. ____ Children learn that it is okay to use violence.

Now listen again. What details are used to explain each cause? Write the number of the cause next to the details.

Details

____ 75% of Americans believe that they will be victims of a violent crime.
____ Violent crime has decreased, but media coverage has increased.
____ Many people buy guns because they feel they need to protect their family.
____ Children have grown used to seeing violence and are no longer shocked by it.
____ The TV media uses the drama of violence to attract viewers.
____ Young people may be influenced by the government's use of violence to resolve conflicts.

Compare your answers with a partner. Then listen again and check.

Brainstorming

First, work in a group to brainstorm a list of interesting and important problems. They can be international, national, or local. Then choose one problem as the topic of a cause/effect speech. Brainstorm *Wh~* questions to generate details about the problem. What is the problem? Who is it a problem for? Where is it a problem? Why should we care about this problem?

Interesting & Important Problems

Who?	**What?**	**Where?**	**When?**	**Why?**

Now brainstorm a list of possible causes of this problem.

Possible Causes

Now show your list to a partner. Which do you think are most likely the real causes? Put a check (✓) next to them.

Gathering Information

Once you've identified some possible causes, it's time to do some research. Find information on your topic. Keep an open mind; you may find some surprises! Find out if the causes you listed are truly the causes. If not, you may need to revise your list. Find details about three possible causes and write the information below.

Speech Key 8.3

Keep an open mind. Allow the facts to guide you as you research causes.

Cause 1	Cause 2	Cause 3

Effective Research I: The Basics

Conducting research is a process of discovery, an opportunity to explore ideas and improve your understanding. You will learn more advanced research skills in later units. These tips will help you get started.

Conducting Research: Getting Started

1. Brainstorm a list of keywords related to your topic.
2. Use a wide variety of sources, including electronic databases, the Internet, and periodicals. Don't rely on only one source.
3. Look for factual information. Don't rely on the opinions of others.
4. Take notes as you find useful information; make copies of important pages or sections.
5. Keep your notes organized. Keep a record of all the sources you find.
6. If you cannot find the sources you need, ask a librarian for help.

Prepare

Now write your speech. Make sure you describe the problem carefully and explain its causes. Also, make sure you have enough factual details to explain each point.

Practice

Work with a partner and practice your speech. Pay careful attention to how emotions are expressed. Also, note the quality of the causes and the details used to support them.

Notes on Expression

What emotions are communicated? ____________

____

____

Are they appropriate? ____________________

____

How could expression be improved? __________

____

Notes on Content

	yes	no
Is the problem clearly explained?	____	____
Are the causes clearly identified?	____	____
Is there enough factual detail?	____	____

Notes for improvement ______________________

____

____

Sound Pronunciation

[ei] This is a long vowel sound.
▶ whale, mail, trade, suede, fate, crave, shade

[ai] This is a short vowel sound.
▶ try, hind, sign, why, strike, wine, spike

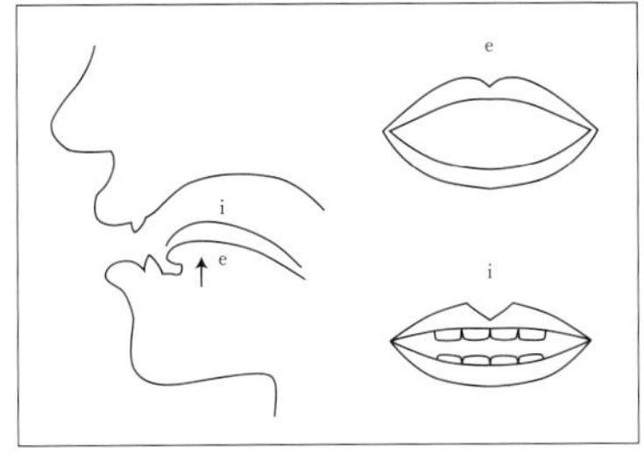

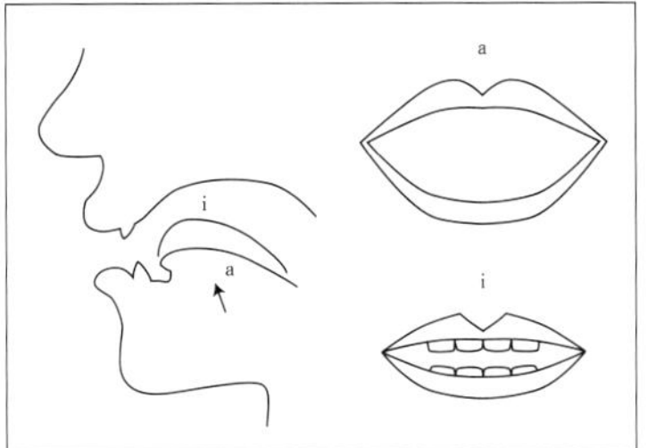

DL 58 CD 1-58
Now, listen to the CD and repeat.

DL 59 CD 1-59

Write "ei" or "ai" on the line to describe the vowel sound. Then listen to the CD and check.

_ei_ great ____ grind ____ hate ____ hail ____ pile ____ stale ____ style
____ mile ____ steak ____ cake ____ mild ____ grail ____ take

Stress for Emphasis

DL 60 CD 1-60

To show enthusiasm or strong feelings, place heavy stress on the main words or syllables. Listen to the CD and repeat. Underline the stressed syllables.

I love this food!
What a wonderful movie!
The ride was so exciting!

You'll never guess what happened!
You have got to see this film!
The test was incredibly difficult!

I couldn't believe what I saw!
We must take action soon!
What would you do in this situation?

Write two more sentences. Practice saying them with a partner, adding stress for emphasis. Then say them to your group or class.

____

____

Grammar Review: Explaining Cause & Effect

There are several grammatical structures we can use to show cause/effect relationships.

Adverb Clauses	Because… Since… Now that…
Transitions	Therefore, …
Simple Connectors	…, so… …for…
Prepositions	because of… due to…

Adverb Clauses
Because I passed the test, I could enter the university.
I could enter the university because I passed the test.
Since the game was canceled, we went to a movie instead.
Now that I have graduated, I want to find a job.

Transitions
Mary gave an excellent speech. Therefore, she got an "A".

Simple Connectors
He stopped exercising, so now he is out of shape.
I can't buy a new car, for I don't have any money.

Prepositions
The public opposed construction because of the noise.
Because of public opposition, construction was stopped.

Use one of the structures above to show the relationship between ideas.
Try to use a different structure in cach sentence you write.

Bob was tired ( ) overwork.
Bob was tired *due to* overwork.

1. I have a headache ( ) I will not go to school today.
____
2. I can't sleep ( ) I'm worried about the test.
____
3. I passed the test ( ) hard work and study.
____
4. I have mastered English ( ) I want to use it in my career.
____
5. The rain stopped, ( ), the game resumed.
____

DL 61 CD 1-61
Compare your answers with a partner. Then listen to the CD and check.

Complete the following sentences.

1. I caught a cold because ____________________.
2. Due to the rain, ____________________.
3. I failed the test. Therefore, ____________________.
4. Now that I am 20, ____________________.
5. I lived in England for two years, so ____________________.
6. Since I speak English well, ____________________.
7. Because ____________________, I'm in really great shape!

DL 62 CD 1-62
Compare your answers with a partner. Then listen to the CD and check.

Unit 9

What Dreams May Come...

Warm-Up

What are your dreams for the future? Put a check (✓) next to the things you would like to do someday:

____ get married ____ become rich ____ learn to fly ____ visit Antarctica ____ drive a Ferrari
____ write a novel ____ become famous ____ own a company ____ be prime minister

Write two more things you would like to do.

Someday, I would like to ____________________.
In the future, I hope to ____________________.

Share your ideas with your group. Ask your classmates questions about their dreams.

How long have you had this dream? How will you accomplish your dream? Why did you choose this dream?

Rhetorical Strategy I: Repetition

When people read, they are free to go back and reread parts they didn't understand the first time. However, a presentation audience cannot do so—they have only one chance to understand. Your job is to lead the audience, ensuring that they can follow your ideas. You can do this with repetition, which is the restatement of key words or ideas at certain points.

Speech Key 9.1

Repeating certain words or phrases can guide your audience and reinforce key points.

Using Repetition to Reinforce Ideas

1. Identify key ideas in your speech that you want to reinforce.
2. Identify words or phrases that communicate those ideas.
3. Find places in your speech where you can repeat those words or phrases.

Using Repetition to Guide the Audience

1. Outline what you are going to say.
2. Say it.
3. Repeat it.

Go to http://www.americanrhetoric.com/speeches/Ihaveadream.htm. Listen to the speech by Dr. Martin Luther King. What words or phrases does he repeat? How many times?

Practice

Look at the following information from a brainstorming activity. What important words or phrases could be used for repetition?

Cleaner energy is good for the environment.
Oil is expensive.
Oil is non-renewable.
Solar power is free.
Solar power is clean.
We are dependent on other countries for oil.
Dependence on imports is dangerous.
Alternative energy makes us safe because we won't be dependent.
There is less chance of war.
Electric cars are clean.
Electric cars are becoming cheaper.
Oil is dirty.
Oil is bad for the environment.
A cleaner environment makes life better.

List three words that are key to organizing the brainstorming list. Work with a partner.

____

____

____

DL 63 CD 1-63

Listen to the CD and check your answers. How many times do you hear each key word? Write one sentence to explain the main idea of this presentation.

____

Building Your Speech: Explaining Reasons

The words "reason" and "cause" are often used synonymously. Both are used to answer the key question, *Why?* We use "causes" to refer to the circumstances leading to results. "Reasons" refer to more personal circumstances leading to beliefs or actions.

Speech Key 9.2

We all have reasons for our beliefs and actions. Earn your audience's respect by explaining your reasons.

Distinguishing reasons from causes. Write "C" in the blank if the statements describe a cause. Write "R" for reasons.

1. Supply is low. → Prices rise. ____
2. I love to travel. → I went to Europe. ____
3. The temperature is below 0°C. → Water freezes. ____
4. I want to improve my English. → I study every day. ____

Look at these possible speech topics. Which ones would be best supported by causes? Which ones require reasons? Write "C" or "R" next to each blank.

____ rising gold prices
____ why I don't want children
____ why Chicago is my favorite city
____ why we should reduce energy use
____ why I became a teacher
____ why I got married
____ why the sky is blue
____ why World War II started
____ global warming
____ the French Revolution

Practice

Listen to the CD. The speaker explains her reasons for wishing to live and work abroad someday.

What are her reasons for wishing to live and work abroad?

1. ______________________
2. ______________________
3. ______________________

What key words or phrases are repeated for reinforcement?

1. ______________________
2. ______________________
3. ______________________

Compare your answers with a partner. Then listen again and check.

Brainstorming

What would you like to do with your life? Brainstorm a list of hopes and dreams for your future. Share your list with your group. Then choose one and brainstorm as many details about it as you can. What is the dream? When did you decide it? Who inspired you? Who is involved in your dream? What must you do to make it come true? When might your dream come true?

My Hopes & Dreams for the Future

____
____
____
____
____

My Dream: Details

____
____
____
____
____

Now brainstorm your reasons for choosing this dream.

My Reasons

____
____
____
____
____

List key words or phrases for repetition.

Key Words & Phrases

____
____
____
____
____

Prepare

Write a short presentation to describe your dream and your reasons for pursuing it. Make sure you use repetition to guide the audience and reinforce key ideas.

Practice

Work with a partner and practice your presentation. Note the main idea and reasons given for pursuing the dream and the use of repetition. Also, note use of body language. Refer to Units 2 through 5 if necessary.

Main idea: ____________________

____

Reasons:

1. ____________________
2. ____________________
3. ____________________

Key Words & Phrases

____

____

____

Suggestions for improvement:

____

____

Notes on Nonverbal Communication

	good	needs improvement
Eye Contact	____	____
Posture	____	____
Gestures	____	____

Suggestions: ____________________

____

Perform & Evaluate

Perform your speech for your classmates. As your classmates perform, follow the example and complete the evaluation chart.

Name	Eye Contact	Posture	Gestures	Reasons	Comments
Momoko Kawano	✗	✓	///	✓	*3 clear reasons, and good repetition of key words. Slouching shoulders and swaying too much.*

Sound Pronunciation

[ɔi] This is two sounds, "ɔ:" and "i".
▶ toy, coy, foil, noise, destroy, voice, boil

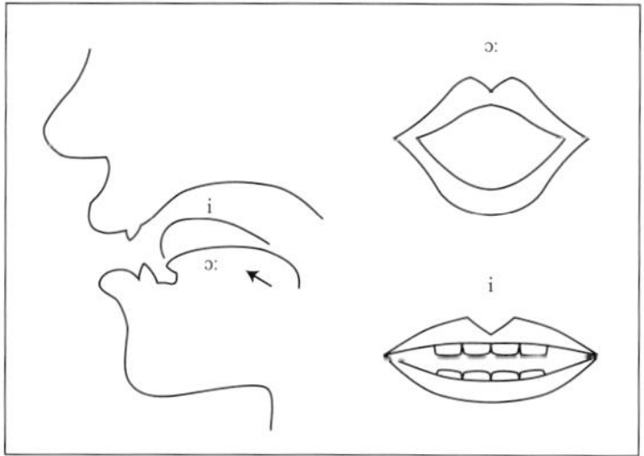

[au] This is a combination of "æ" and "u".
▶ mouse, crowd, house, loud, out, ouch

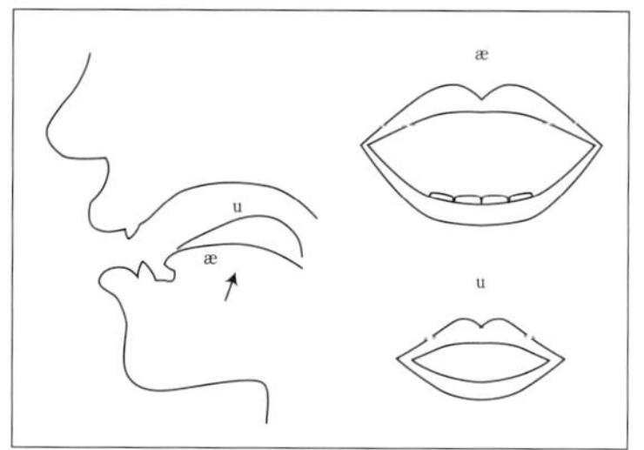

DL 65 CD 1-65
Now, listen to the CD and repeat.

DL 66 CD 1-66
Write "ɔi" or "au" on the line to describe the vowel sound. Then listen to the CD and check.

_ɔi_ joy ____ rout ____ shout ____ coil ____ coin ____ doubt ____ owl
____ employ ____ Joyce ____ choice ____ down ____ frown ____ trounce

Stress for Clarity

In natural speech, the word *to* is pronounced "tə". Listen to the CD and repeat. DL 67 CD 1-67

I'd like to travel for a year after I graduate.
I plan to start a family in my twenties.
I wish to become rich.
I hope to start my own business someday.
I'd love to live in the big city.
I'd love to!*

Note: If *to* comes at the end of the sentence, it is fully pronounced.

The "t" sound in *want to* and *going to* is barely heard. Listen to the CD and repeat. DL 68 CD 1-68

I want to study abroad this summer.
I want to go to graduate school next year.
I'm going to take a test tomorrow.
I'm going to be prime minister someday.*

Note: The "t" sound is heard clearly if *want to* or *going to* is stressed.

Grammar Review: Expressing Future Time

There are several grammatical structures we can use to show future time, with slight differences in meaning.

Form	*going to* + verb	*will* + verb	*may/might* + verb	*want to* *wish to* *hope to* + verb *plan to* *would like to/love to*
Use	Often used to express certainty or a firm decision to do something.	Often used to express immediate action or spontaneous decisions.	Used to express a lower degree of certainty; something not decided firmly.	Used to express dreams, goals, and desires.
Negative	*not going to* + verb	*will not* + verb	*may not/might not* + verb	*do not want/wish/ hope/plan to* + verb
Examples	I'm going to buy a new car. I'm not going to go to work tomorrow.	(phone rings) I'll get it. A: We're out of milk. B: I'll buy some more. I will not listen anymore.	I might go to Europe next year, but I'm not sure. I may not pass the test next week.	I don't want to take the test. I wish to master English. I hope to marry a rich woman. I plan to get a job after college. I'd love to make a lot of money.

*Note: It is possible to use *may* or *might to* express uncertainty in the present. Ex. Tom may be sick today.

Fill in the blanks with future forms to reflect your own feelings.

I hope to get married before I am 30 years old.

1. I ____________ live and work in a foreign country.
2. I ____________ retire before I am 50 years old.
3. I ____________ have more than 4 children.
4. I ____________ be my own boss.
5. I ____________ go skydiving someday.
6. I ____________ use English in my career.
7. I ____________ become rich and famous.
8. I ____________ live in the countryside.
9. I ____________ live in a big city.
10. I ____________ take a vacation next summer.

Unit 10 For Example...

Warm-Up

Listen to the CD. You will hear a presentation about wedding parties in the US and in Japan. How are they different? How are they the same? Next to each item, write "US" if it is a feature of US weddings, write "J" if it is a feature of Japanese weddings, and write "B" if it is common to both.

DL 69 CD 2-01

____ Dancing ____ Friends and Family Attend ____ Best Man's Toast

____ Boss's Toast ____ Drinking ____ Throwing Rice or Birdseed

Put a check (✓) next to the examples used for support.

____ His Sister's Wedding ____ His Best Friend's Wedding

____ His Japanese Co-Worker's Wedding ____ His Brother's Wedding

Compare your answers with a partner. Then listen again and check.

Rhetorical Strategy II: Using Simple Language

Long, complex sentences and uncommon words are acceptable in written English because the reader can go back and reread difficult parts. But the audience for your speech cannot do so; you have only one chance to communicate. Avoid using words your audience may not understand. Keep your sentences short and simple.

Look at the uncommon words on the left. Match them to their more common synonyms on the right.

inchoate	short-sighted
saturnine	sorrowful, mournful
static	double-dealing, deceitful
myopic	undeveloped, immature
lugubrious	balanced, stable
duplicitous	gloomy

Find a More Common Synonym for These Words:

verbose

____

fallacious

____

circumspect

____

Speech Key 10.1

Keep it simple! Big words won't make you look smarter. They only confuse your audience.

Simple Rules for Simple Language

1. Avoid using jargon.
2. Avoid uncommon acronyms.
3. Don't clutter a sentence with too many ideas.
4. Use familiar words when possible.
5. Choose concrete words over abstract words.
6. Keep sentence structure as simple as possible.

Practice

Rewrite the following sentences to make them easier to understand.

There are many students of this university who are planning to attend the lecture which is to be held next week.

Many university students plan to attend next week's lecture.

1. Trouble is the result when people do not obey the rules that have been established for the safety of everyone.

____

2. She was forced to withdraw from the university as a result of the fact that it was necessary to earn money.

____

3. It is expected that the university will make an announcement about the schedule for next year within the next few days.

____

Compare your answers with a partner. Then listen to the model answers on the CD. DL 70 CD 2-02

Practice

Listen to the CD. You will hear excerpts of two versions of the same presentation. Check (✓) "A" or "B" to indicate which uses simpler language. DL 71 

1. ____ A ____ B 2. ____ A ____ B 3. ____ A ____ B
4. ____ A ____ B 5. ____ A ____ B 6. ____ A ____ B

Compare your answers with a partner. Listen again and check.

Building Your Speech: Using Examples

In Unit 7 we learned about facts—the most common and powerful type of support. But sometimes facts are not enough. Examples can make our ideas clearer.

Speech Key 10.2

Examples help your audience understand complex or abstract ideas.

Match the idea on the left with the appropriate example on the right.

1. Japanese food is very healthy.
2. DNA evidence is a powerful tool for defense lawyers.
3. After school programs can keep kids out of trouble.
4. You don't need to be rich to be happy.
5. Schooling is only one part of your education.

a. In Chicago, youth crime dropped by 50% when a new after school basketball program was introduced.
b. Sushi contains a variety of important nutrients and is a good source of protein.
c. In Los Angeles, students do volunteer work to learn about the value of community.
d. Analysis of John Murphey's hair proved that he could not have been the killer.
e. My Uncle Joe earns a very low salary as a bus driver, but he loves his job and has little stress.

Practice

Listen to the CD. You will hear a short presentation comparing Japanese and American universities. Put a check (✓) next to the key points the speaker makes. Then draw a line to match the key point to the example used for support.

	Key point		Example
____	American professors are often stricter.	a.	Some professors allow students to miss class only once.
____	Club activities are more popular in Japan.	b.	Only 60% of my freshman class was able to graduate after four years.
____	Students in both countries often have part-time jobs.	c.	I worked as a waiter at a restaurant, and so do many of my Japanese students.
____	It may be more difficult to graduate from US universities.	d.	When I was a student, I made many close friends as a member of the rugby club.

Compare your answers with a partner. Then listen again and check.

Brainstorming: Comparison & Contrast

When we compare things or ideas, we look for ways in which they are the same or similar. When we contrast things or ideas, we look for ways in which they are different.
Work with a partner and brainstorm a list of possible topics for a comparison/contrast presentation. Use the list of subjects below to help you get started.

Possible Subjects for Comparison/Contrast

cities	religions	customs	movies
cars	cuisine	fashions	cultures
sports	musicians	restaurants	careers
actors	presidents	writers	countries

Topics for Comparison/Contrast

American and Japanese Weddings

Tokyo and New York

____

____

____

____

____

____

____

____

Choose one topic. How are these things or ideas similar? How are they different? Start by brainstorming as many details as possible. Then organize the details according to similarities and differences.

Topic: ________ and ________	**Similarities**	**Differences**

Building Your Speech: Patterns of Organization

There are several possible patterns of organization for a comparison/contrast presentation. Listen again to the CD. Put a check (✓) next to the pattern that was used. Then choose one pattern and outline your own presentation.

DL 73 CD 2-05

____ Pattern 1: Explain one, then the other

I. Introduction
II. Japanese Universities
III. American Universities
IV. Similarities and Differences

____ Pattern 2: First Compare, then Contrast

I. Introduction
II. How American and Japanese U. are the same.
III. How they are different.
IV. Conclusion

____ Pattern 3: Element by Element

I. Introduction
II. The Professors
III. Working
IV. Graduating

Outline: Comparison/Contrast

Topic: ____________________

____
____
____
____
____
____
____
____
____

Prepare

Prepare a presentation in which you compare and contrast two things or ideas. Make sure to support your key points with examples.

Practice

Work with a partner and practice your presentation. Take notes to help your partner make improvements.

Notes on Language

	yes	no
Uncommon words	____	____
Cluttered ideas	____	____
Long sentences	____	____
Unusual acronyms	____	____

Notes for improvement: ____________________

____

Notes on Examples

Idea: ____________________

Supporting example: ____________________

____

Idea: ____________________

Supporting example: ____________________

____

Suggestions for improvement: ____________________

____

Sound Pronunciation

[iə] This is a combination of two sounds, "i" and "ə".
▸ hear, steer, pier, clear, beard, fear, jeer

[eə] This is a combination of "e" and "ə".
▸ hair, care, stair, chair, wear, bear, air

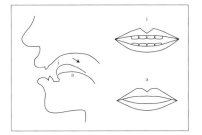

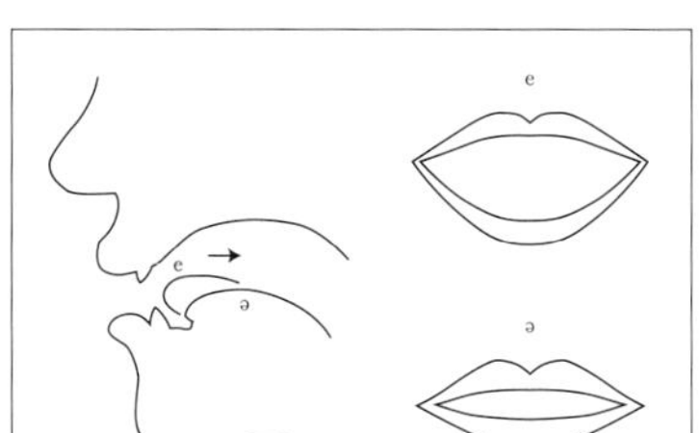

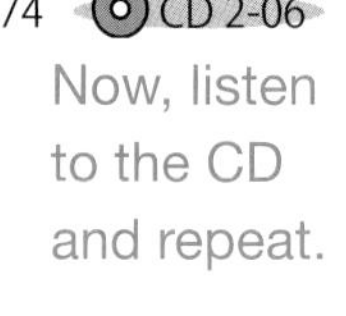

Now, listen to the CD and repeat.

Write "iə" or "eə" on the line to describe the vowel sound. Then listen to the CD and check.

_iə_ smear ____ cheer ____ dare ____ square ____ dear ____ bare ____ beer
____ fair ____ where ____ steer ____ stare ____ mare ____ near

Stress for Clarity: Emphasis on Content Words

In English, content words, or words that contain the most meaning, usually carry more stress. Structure words receive less emphasis. The contrast helps your audience remember the important information.

Content Words	Structure Words
nouns main verbs adverbs adjectives question words	pronouns prepositions articles conjunctions "be" verbs modals

Listen to the CD and repeat during the pauses. Notice the stress. DL 76 CD 2-08

1. Have you decided what you'd like to eat?
2. How long have you been waiting?
3. Students pay a lot of money for textbooks.
4. Old English is difficult to understand.
5. What is the capital of Montana?

Grammar Review: Making Comparisons

There are several ways to make comparisons in English.

Form	*the same (as)* *similar (to)* *different (from)*	N + *be* + *like* + N *(similar to)* N and N + *be* + *alike (similar)*	adjective + *er* *more/less* + adjective *better/worse/farther/further**
Examples	This is the same as that. This class and that class are the same. Canada is similar to America. Canada and America are similar. My brother and I are different. I am different from my brother.	His hat is like my hat. His hat and my hat are alike. Bob's car is like my car. My car and Bob's car are alike.	Tokyo is bigger than Osaka. Tokyo is bigger. New York is more interesting than Ohio. Ohio is less interesting. Your cooking is better than mine. My cooking is worse.

* Irregular forms.

Change these adjectives to their comparative forms.

young *younger*

1. important ____________
2. easy ____________
3. difficult ____________
4. boring ____________
5. fine ____________
6. good ____________
7. thin ____________
8. famous ____________
9. happy ____________
10. exciting ____________

Fill in the blanks with *the same (as), similar (to)*, or *different (from)*.

✔	×	♣	❤	✯	❖	❖	→	➡	☆	☆	→	✓	✘	✳	✳
A	B	C	D	E	F	G	H	I	J	K	L	M	N	O	P

1. A is ____________ M.
2. F is ____________ G.
3. A and J are ____________.
4. H and I are ____________.
5. J and K are ____________.
6. D and O are ____________.
7. E and K are ____________.
8. C is ____________ P.

Fill in the blanks with *like* or *alike*.

1. A is ____________ M.
2. E and K are ____________.
3. O and P are ____________.
4. H is ____________ I.

Compare your answers with a partner. Then listen to the CD and check. DL 77 CD 2-09

Unit 11

Make a Stand, Hold Your Ground!

Warm-Up

What do you think about these controversial positions? Where do you stand?
Write "Yes" next to statements you agree with; write "No" if you disagree.

____ Women are better leaders than men.
____ Children should be taught English in elementary school.
____ College students should not work at part-time jobs.
____ Good English is necessary to compete in a global economy.
____ We should have tougher laws against public smoking.

Now, write one position of your own. Discuss them with your group.

____

Rhetorical Strategy III: Using the Active Voice

We can make sentences with three basic verb structures:

1. The active voice: Where the subject is the main focus.
   The Yankees won the World Series.
2. The passive voice: Where the object is the main focus.
   The World Series was won by the Yankees.
3. Linking verbs: The *be* verbs is used to link ideas.
   The Yankees were the World Series winners.

Of course you must use linking verbs sometimes. It would be very difficult to speak at length without using *is, are, am, was,* or *were.* Sometimes the passive voice is appropriate, especially when you want to de-emphasize the subject (ex. *Mistakes were made.*). Generally, however, you should try to use the active voice whenever possible.

Speech Key 11.1

Be Active!
The active voice is more powerful, interesting and memorable.

Why Use the Active Voice?

The active voice...

1. is more direct.
2. makes sentences that are shorter and easier to follow.
3. is more forceful.
4. creates more memorable images.
5. is more interesting.

Rewrite the following sentences, changing the structure from the passive to the active voice.

1. *Ulysses* was written by James Joyce. ______________________
2. The moon was first set foot upon by Neil Armstrong. ______________________

Practice

Rewrite the following speech. Change the structure to the active voice whenever possible.

The World is Changed by Volunteer Work!

The neediest people are helped by volunteers. For example, people with no food are fed by volunteers. People with no home are housed by homeless shelters. Also, people who cannot read are taught by volunteers. Volunteer programs are started and supported by local communities. Needs are assessed by community leaders, and programs are developed by organizers, but your help is needed by them. By volunteering just a few hours per month, your community can be made stronger by you. And a strong sense of connection to your community and accomplishment can be felt by you. Furthermore, the benefits are enjoyed by everyone. Little by little, the world is changed by volunteer work. Be a part of it!

Volunteer Work Changes the World!

____

____

____

____

____

____

____

____

Now listen to the CD. Compare your version of the speech to the one you hear. DL 78 CD 2-10

Practice

Listen to the CD. You will hear ten sentences. Write "A" if the sentence is active, "P" for passive, or "L" if a linking verb is used. DL 79 CD 2-11

1. ____ 2. ____ 3. ____ 4. ____ 5. ____ 6. ____ 7. ____ 8. ____ 9. ____ 10. ____

Compare your answers with a partner. Then listen again and check.

Building Your Speech: Finding Good Reasons

It is not enough to have reasons. To communicate your opinion to an audience, you need relevant reasons that can be supported with evidence. People may not agree with you, but they can understand and respect your opinion.

Speech Key 11.2

There is no such thing as a "wrong" opinion. But by offering good reasons and solid support, you will earn respect, even from people who disagree.

Read the following position. Then, circle the best reason in support of it.

I believe the Yankees will win the World Series this year.

a. They have great uniforms. b. They have great hitting and pitching.
c. They have a great history.

Practice

Read the following positions. Then put a check (✓) next to the reason that best supports the position.

1. Tokyo is the best city to live in.
   ____ It is the cultural center of Japan.
   ____ I like Tokyo.
   ____ Tokyo is the largest city in Japan.

2. Japanese food is very healthy.
   ____ There is a great variety of Japanese food.
   ____ It contains a variety of vitamins.
   ____ Japanese food is delicious.

3. The Prime Minister should be elected by the Japanese people.
   ____ The President is elected by the people in the US.
   ____ Prime Minister Koizumi was not elected by the people.
   ____ Direct election would increase accountability.

4. Junk food should not be served in school cafeterias.
   ____ Junk food is cheaper than healthy food.
   ____ Junk food is popular because it is convenient and tasty.
   ____ Junk food can cause a variety of health problems.

Compare your answers with a partner. Explain why some reasons are better than others.

Practice

Listen to the CD. You will hear two short speeches on the topic of cram schools. First, write down each person's position and reasons. Then put a check next to the speech that is supported by better reasons.

online video DL 80 CD 2-12

Speech 1 ____
Position: ____________________
Reasons:
1. ____________________
2. ____________________
3. ____________________

Speech 2 ____
Position: ____________________
Reasons:
1. ____________________
2. ____________________
3. ____________________

Compare your answers with a partner. Then listen again and check.

Brainstorming

Brainstorm a list of possible topics for a speech in which you support your position with appropriate reasons.

List of Possible Topics

____
____
____
____

Share your list with a group and discuss your positions.

Next, choose one topic, write your position, and make a list of possible reasons for your position.

Topic: ______________ Position: ______________
Reasons:
1. ____________________
2. ____________________
3. ____________________
4. ____________________

Show your reasons to your group. Together decide which three reasons are the best.

Building Your Speech: Patterns of Organization

Reasons support positions, and evidence supports reasons. By following this simple structure, your audience can easily follow your ideas.

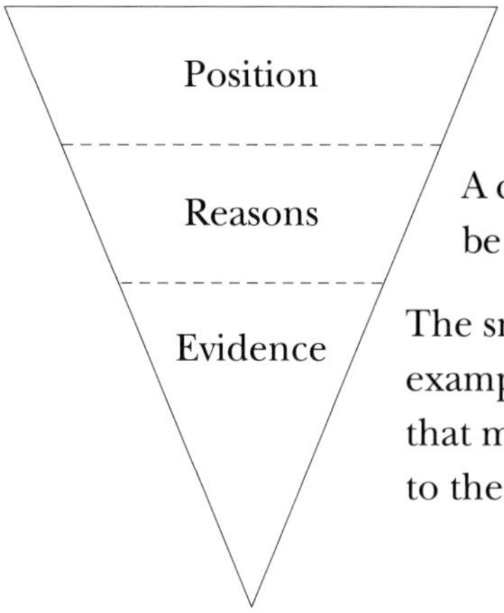

Position — A general statement of your idea.

Reasons — A cause for belief or action; should be relevant and supportable.

Evidence — The small details—facts, examples, and explanations that make your reasons clear to the audience.

Now write a speech in which you take a position on a topic. Find three good reasons for your position and support each reason with evidence. You may need to go to the library to find evidence to support your reasons.

Position Speech Outline

Topic: ______________________________

Position: ______________________________

Reason 1: ______________________________

____

Evidence: ______________________________

____

____

Reason 2: ______________________________

____

Evidence: ______________________________

____

____

Reason 3: ______________________________

____

Evidence: ______________________________

____

____

Prepare

Prepare a speech about a controversial topic. Make sure to take a clear position, support your position with good reasons, and support your reasons with good evidence. Remember to use simple language and the active voice as much as possible.

Practice

Work with a partner to practice your speech. Pay close attention to the quality of the reasons given. Also, help ensure that your partner uses the active voice.

Notes on Reasons

	relevant? yes	no
Reason 1: ______________	____	____
Reason 2: ______________	____	____
Reason 3: ______________	____	____
Does evidence support each reason?	____	____

Suggestions: ______________________________

____

____

Notes on the Active Voice

Active verbs used: ______________________________

____

Passive verbs used: ______________________________

____

Linking verbs used: ______________________________

____

Suggestions for improvement:

____

____

Sound Pronunciation

[əu] Our final vowel sound is a combination of "ə" and "u".
▶ boat, home, loan, known, bone, bowl, toll

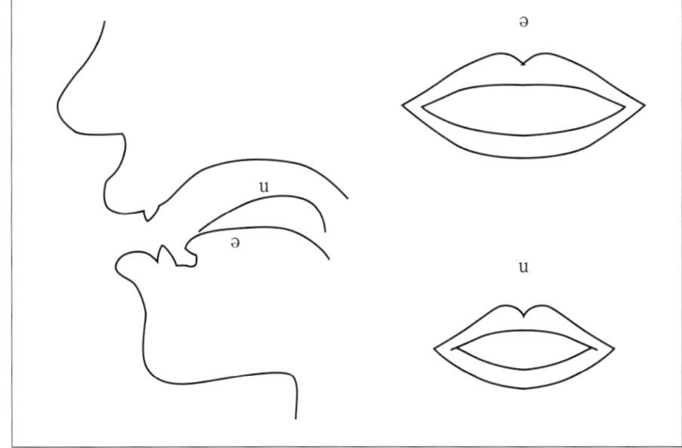

Now, listen to the CD and repeat. DL 81 CD 2-13

DL 82 CD 2-14
Write "uː," "u," "ɔi," "ɑu," or "əu" on the line to describe each vowel sound. Review Units 5 & 9 if necessary. Then listen to the CD and check.

____ shoot ____ look ____ coy ____ show ____ mouse ____ shook ____ route ____ boil
____ bowl ____ howl ____ loyal ____ clone ____ drool ____ ouch ____ good

Stress for Clarity: General Rules

Rule 1: In every two-syllable word, one syllable will carry stress, while the other will not.

báseball Japán áctor cóffee

Rule 2: In all words with three or more syllables, the following applies:
a. One syllable will carry the main stress; marked with ˊ.
b. Some syllables will carry secondary stress; marked with ˋ.
c. Some syllables will be reduced and barely heard.

3-syllable	4-syllable	5-syllable	6-syllable
Hóllywòod	prèposítion	prèdóminantly	gèneralizátion
reáction	èconómic	pùrificátion	idèntificátion
detérmine	scìentífic	òrientátion	ìnternátionalize
ópposite	Ìndiána	àstronómical	ùninhíbited

DL 83 CD 2-15
Listen to the CD and repeat.

Listen to the CD and mark the main and secondary stress in each of these words. DL 84 CD 2-16

pioneer participation official individualize electricity incoherent incompatible proficient ludicrous necessity priority organizational incontrovertible idiosyncratic transformation elastic gratitude interdependence

Compare your answers with a partner. Then listen again and repeat.

Grammar Review: Active and Passive Verbs

All verb forms can be changed from active to passive and passive to active.
Basic form of passive: be + past participle.

Verb Form	Active	Passive
simple present	Bill cooks dinner.	Dinner is cooked by Bill.
simple past	Bill cooked dinner.	Dinner was cooked by Bill.
present perfect	Bill has cooked dinner.	Dinner has been cooked by Bill.
past progressive	Bill was cooking dinner.	Dinner was being cooked by Bill.
past perfect	Bill had cooked dinner.	Dinner had been cooked by Bill.
future	Bill will cook dinner.	Dinner will be cooked by Bill.
future perfect	Bill will have cooked dinner.	Dinner will have been cooked by Bill.

*Note: Only transitive verbs can be made passive. If there is no direct object in the active form, it cannot be changed to passive.

Change the following sentences from active to passive. One of them cannot be changed.

1. Laurie plays guitar. ____________________
2. Bryan ate grapes. ____________________
3. George has taken the test. ____________________
4. Marian was drinking wine. ____________________
5. Mike had never tried sushi. ____________________
6. John will buy a truck. ____________________
7. Katie is going to be a star. ____________________
8. Connor will have learned French. ____________________
9. Olivia is going to sing a song. ____________________

Change the following sentences from passive to active.

1. English is spoken by Laurie. ____________________
2. A fight was won by Bryan. ____________________
3. A test has been failed by George. ____________________
4. A waltz has been danced by Marian. ____________________
5. A letter has been sent by Mike. ____________________
6. A dish will be prepared by John. ____________________
7. Lunch is going to be served by Katie. ____________________
8. The door will have been locked by Connor. ____________________
9. The lessons are going to be learned by Olivia. ____________________

Compare your answers with a partner. Then listen to the CD and check. DL 85 CD 2-17

Unit 12

Measuring Solutions, Solving Problems

Warm-Up

Look at the list of problems below. Match them to two possible solutions on the right.

Global Warming Caused by Cars
Juvenile Delinquency
Social Security for an Aging Society

____ After school programs for young people.
____ Destroy all automobiles.
____ Raise taxes to pay for social security.
____ Limit the amount of pollution cars can make.
____ Make stronger penalties for youth crime.
____ Reduce social security benefits.

Put a check (✓) next to the solution for each problem that you think is best.

Here is another problem. Try to think of two possible solutions.

Problem: In elementary schools, the incidence of bullying has increased in recent years.

Solution 1: ______________________________

Solution 2: ______________________________

Rhetorical Strategy IV: The Rule of Three

Your goal is to make a lasting impression on your audience so that they will remember the key points of your speech long after it is over. However, in reality, your audience will probably remember only three points. Therefore, choose them carefully, phrase them simply, and repeat them to make them memorable!

Speech Key 12.1

Think "Three"! Your audience is likely to remember only three key points from your presentation. Make them memorable.

Bob is a car salesman, and he must persuade an audience of powerful, wealthy men to buy a Flexus sports car. All of the following points are true. Which three points do you think would be most persuasive for this audience?

____ Luxury
____ Powerful engine
____ Stability
____ Reliability
____ Easy to drive
____ Good gas mileage
____ Famous people drive it
____ Gracefulness

DL 86 CD 2-18

Now listen to the CD. Did you choose the same three points as Bob?

Practice

Your audience will remember three key points, and your final point will be the most memorable. Therefore, save the best for last!

Speech Key 12.1

Save the best for last! The final main point of your speech will be the most memorable.

In each situation you must persuade an audience. Brainstorm a list of three points you could make to persuade the audience. Save the best for last.

Context: You are applying for a study abroad scholarship.
Audience: The scholarship committee, which selects the winner.
Task: Persuade them that you deserve the scholarship.

1. ____________________
2. ____________________
3. ____________________

Context: You are applying for a job as a salesperson with a major computer company.
Audience: The company president who will hire only one person.
Task: Persuade him to hire you.

1. ____________________
2. ____________________
3. ____________________

Context: You are in love. You want your partner to marry you.
Audience: Your skeptical partner.
Task: Persuade her/him that you will be a great husband/wife.

1. ____________________
2. ____________________
3. ____________________

Compare your list with others in your group. Then choose one of the contexts and prepare a short speech.

Building Your Speech: Evaluating Evidence

How do you know if your evidence is good? When evaluating evidence, there are three questions to ask.

Is the Evidence Credible?

If the evidence is likely to surprise your audience, make sure you have a credible source—an expert or authority.

X My father believes there is life on other planets.
✓ NASA scientists believe there may be life on other planets.

Is the Evidence Accurate?

Does the evidence tell the truth? Never mislead your audience or alter information to suit your needs. Use verifiable information honestly.

X My opponent voted for higher taxes 35 times.
✓ My opponent voted for two bills that would increase taxes for 35 different projects.

Is the Evidence Sufficient?

Is there enough evidence to support your ideas? To decide if your evidence is sufficient, think about your audience:

1. What does the audience already know about this point?
2. What does the audience need to know to be convinced?

The less your audience knows, the more evidence you will need.

Practice

Read this excerpt from a speech on global warming. Draw a line through the two sentences that are not from credible sources. Then write the number for the evidence below that would best support each point.

> ... So clearly, global warming is a serious problem that affects us all. But what should we do about it? I suggest that we raise the price of gasoline to $5 per gallon. This solution will help stop global warming in three ways. First, people will drive their cars less, thus adding less CO² to the atmosphere. ____ Second, the extra money can be used to develop alternative fuels. My friend Joe believes that solar power could replace fossil fuels within 20 years. ____ And third, it will make people aware that we face a serious crisis. ____ A poll of my classmates shows that 95% believe global warming is serious. Therefore, if we want to solve the problem of global warming, we should raise the price of gasoline dramatically.

1. According to a study by the Institute for Energy Independence, we could have clean and cheap alternatives to fossil fuels within 20 years if we invested more money into research.
2. A survey of 1,000 Americans revealed that most people don't understand that automobiles are a major source of greenhouse gasses.
3. Right now, gasoline is very cheap—about $2.50 per gallon. By doubling the price, people will plan more carefully to reduce the number of trips they make.

Compare your answers with a partner. Then listen to the CD and check.

Brainstorming

Make a list of serious problems that need to be solved. Note if they are global, national, or local problems. Compare lists in your group.

Serious Problems

Global Warming (global) ______________________

______________________ ______________________

______________________ ______________________

______________________ ______________________

Choose one problem and brainstorm a list of possible causes. Then do some research to find the most likely cause of the problem.

Problem: ______________________

Possible causes:

1. ______________________
2. ______________________
3. ______________________

Once you have identified the likely cause, brainstorm a list of possible solutions. Then do some research to find the best solution.

Likely cause: ______________________

Possible solutions:

1. ______________________
2. ______________________
3. ______________________

Patterns of Organization: Problem Solving

When arguing for a solution to a problem, organize your ideas strategically to persuade your audience.

1. State the problem and explain it. Why should the audience care about this problem?
2. State the cause and explain it.
3. State the solution you think is best and explain it.
4. Make three main points about why this solution is best and provide evidence for each.

Listen to the CD and fill in the outline. DL 88 CD 2-20

Problem Solving Speech

Problem: ____________	Point 1: ____________
Explanation: ____________	Evidence: ____________
____________	____________
Likely Cause: ____________	Point 2: ____________
Explanation: ____________	Evidence: ____________
____________	____________
Best Solution: ____________	Point 3: ____________
Explanation: ____________	Evidence: ____________
____________	____________

Prepare

Prepare your own speech using the same pattern of organization as explained above. Go to the library to gather information. As you argue for a solution, stress three key points.

Practice

Practice with a partner. Evaluate your partner's use of the rule of three and the quality of the evidence by marking each line with "X" or "O." Suggest improvements. Also, evaluate the structure of the speech.

The Rule of Three & Evidence

	point 1	point 2	point 3
Description?	____	____	____
Relevant?	____	____	____
Repeated?	____	____	____
Convincing?	____	____	____
EVIDENCE			
Credible?	____	____	____
Accurate?	____	____	____
Sufficient?	____	____	____

Suggestions for improvement: ____________

____

Notes on Structure

	yes	no
1. Is the problem explained?	____	____
2. Will the audience understand?	____	____
3. Is/Are the cause(s) explained?	____	____
4. Is the solution explained?	____	____
5. Three key points defined?	____	____
6. Three key points supported?	____	____

Suggestions for improvement: ____________

____

____

____

____

Sound Pronunciation

[θ] Place your tongue between your teeth and blow out between your tongue and upper teeth.
▸ theater, thief, thin, with, theme, thesis

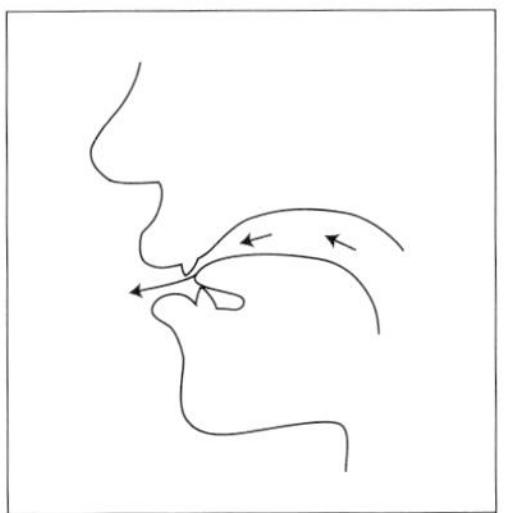

[ð] Same as "θ", but voice the sound by pushing air up from your throat.
▸ weather, they, those, lather, them, bathe

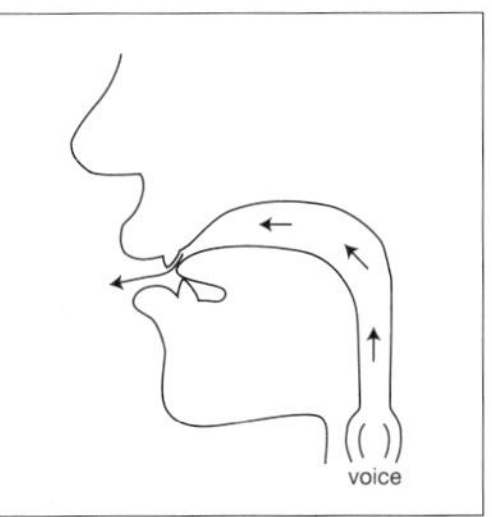

DL 89 CD 2-21
Now, listen to the CD and repeat.

DL 90 CD 2-22

Write "θ" or "ð" on the line to describe the vowel sound. Then listen to the CD and check.

ð that ____ thanks ____ therapy ____ feather ____ death ____ thick ____ this
____ Theodore ____ either ____ ether ____ breathe ____ bother ____ cloth

Stress for Clarity: Using Suffixes to Predict Stress

Certain suffixes usually carry the stress.

~ee	employee	lessee	divorcee
~eer	volunteer	career	mountaineer
~ese	Japanese	Chinese	Vietnamese
~ique	technique	antique	oblique

Some words are likely to have stress on the second syllable before the suffix.

~ize	apologize	criticize	prioritize
~ous	fabulous	perilous	serious
~ate	adequate	educate	exaggerate
~ous	mysterious	furious	spontaneous

In other cases, the stress usually comes right before the suffix.

~ial	essential	financial	burial
~ual	unusual	individual	visual
~ian	politician	librarian	Canadian
~tion	situation	invitation	oration
~sion	occasion	persuasion	conclusion
~cient	proficient	efficient	sufficient
~tious	ambitious	fictitious	cautious
~cious	delicious	suspicious	salacious
~ic	terrific	academic	realistic
~ify	clarify	sanctify	terrify
~ity	calamity	generosity	ability
~graphy	geography	photography	biography
~logy	biology	astrology	psychology
~meter	parameter	kilometer	thermometer

Listen to the CD and repeat. Then look at your problem-solving speech again and practice predicting stress by looking at any suffixes you have included. DL 91 CD 2-23

Grammar Review: Conditionals

When stating solutions, you may need to use conditional structures to express your ideas. Conditional sentences are made up of two clauses: 1. Condition, or *if*-clause; 2. Result, or main clause. The verb form used in each clause depends on the meaning you wish to convey.

Real Conditions	Habitual	Prediction
Verb Form	*If*-clause: present Main clause: present	*If*-clause: present Main clause: modal
Example	If interest rates rise, house prices fall.	If interest rates rise, I will buy a house.

Unreal Conditions	Present or Future Time
Verb Form	*If*-clause: past or could Main clause: past modal (*would, could, might*)
Example	If we raised the price of gasoline, people would drive less.

Match the *if*-clause with the appropriate main clause on the right.

1. If you studied English for three hours every day,
2. If the temperature dips below zero degrees Celsius,
3. If I win a million dollars,
4. If we provide students with computers,
5. If children exercise and sleep well,
6. If I graduated college,
7. If I could travel back through time,
8. If we enact tough gun laws,

- I could get a better job.
- I will retire immediately.
- I would visit my great grandfather.
- it would improve very quickly.
- the violent crime rate will decrease.
- water freezes.
- they will become more technologically savvy.
- they might perform better in school.

Write your own conditional sentences.

1. Real Habitual: ______________________________
2. Real Possibility: ______________________________
3. Unreal: ______________________________

Unit 13

Lies & Statistics...

Warm-Up

Match each claim on the left with its supporting statistical evidence on the right.

- Population growth must be much higher in developing countries.
- Using a computer may actually make you smarter.
- Violent crime should be less of a concern than it was 30 years ago.
- It must be very difficult to make a new restaurant successful.

- In 1974, there were 48 victims of violent crime per 1,000 people. Today, there are 21.1 victims per 1,000 people.
- Students who are computer literate score an average of 20 points higher on I.Q. tests.
- 3 out of 4 new restaurants fail in the first year.
- In 2005, the fertility rate in Japan dropped to 1.25. In Africa, the overall fertility rate is 5.4.

Look at the following statistics. What conclusions can you draw from them? How certain are you?

Women have 65% fewer automobile accidents than men. ______________________________.

Smoking accounts for 80% of lung cancer cases. ______________________________.

Appeals I: Appealing to Character

You may have a strong argument, but if your character is in doubt, your audience is unlikely to trust you.

Speech Key 13.1

Your reputation is your greatest asset. Be reasonable, honest, and thorough.

How to Establish Character

1. Be well-prepared. You will feel confident and competent.
2. Look good! Sloppy dress and messy hair is certain to raise doubts among your audience.
3. Create empathy by showing that you understand and respect the values of your audience.
4. Use evidence honestly and explain it fully. Never manipulate statistics for your own purposes.
5. Avoid manipulating emotions. Though emotional appeals are sometimes appropriate, use them carefully.
6. Consider all sides of an issue. Be thorough and fair.
7. Listen to your audience! Answer their questions.

First impressions are important. By dressing appropriately and having good hygiene, you begin to establish credibility.

Practice

The following opening statements show an awareness of the values of a particular audience and establish empathy. Match the statements on the left by writing the number next to the intended audience on the right.

1. Let me start by saying that I share your concern for the safety and education of all the children in our community.
2. I'm sure you are as concerned as I am about the recent drop in share prices.
3. I know that rising tuition costs and reduced financial aid are creating a burden for you.
4. I know the rising costs of teaching staff and reduced support from the state have made tuition hikes necessary.
5. I, too, have witnessed the devastating effects of crime on our neighborhoods.
6. We all share a sense of loss that James is no longer with us.

____ University Students
____ Parent/Teacher Association
____ Company Shareholders
____ Funeral Attendees
____ Community Association
____ University Administrators

DL 92 CD 2-24

Listen to the CD. Notice how tone is used to establish empathy.

Building Your Speech: Creating Visual Aids

They say a picture is worth 1,000 words. That's because visual images are easier to remember than spoken words or numbers. Simple but powerful visual aids will make your presentation much more effective.

Keys to Creating Effective Visual Aids

1. Keep it simple. Don't try to cram too much information into one visual aid.
2. Make it large. Follow the 8H rule. Generally, visual aids are readable at a distance of 8 times their height. So, if your image is 1 meter tall, your audience should be able to see it from 8 meters away.
3. Avoid distractions. Too many graphics, fonts, and colors can overwhelm the audience.
4. Remember that visual aids support the presentation—they don't comprise it. Don't overuse visual aids.

Speech Key 13.2

Presentations supported with visual aids are 43% more effective than presentations without visual aids.

Types of Visual Aids and Their Uses

Type	Use
Line Graphs	Show changes over time.
Bar Graphs	Compare data.
Pie Charts	Show relationships between percentages.
Organizational Charts	Illustrate hierarchies or structural patterns.
Flow Charts	Demonstrate steps in a process.
Outlines	Highlight key points for the audience.
Props	Add a physical sense to the presentation.

Practice

Identify the type of visual aid.

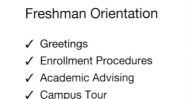

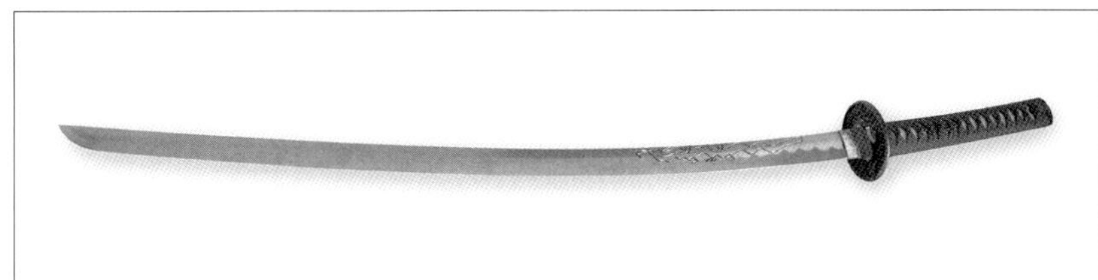

1. ______________________

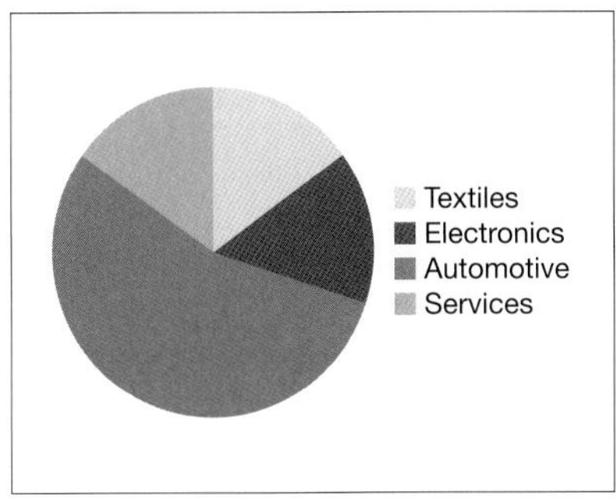

2. ______________________

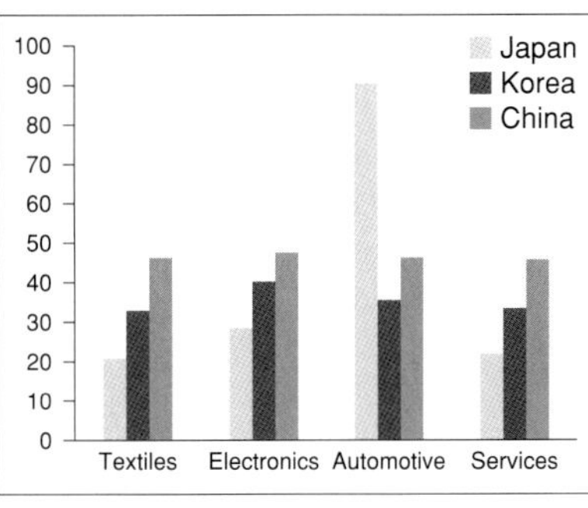

3. ______________________

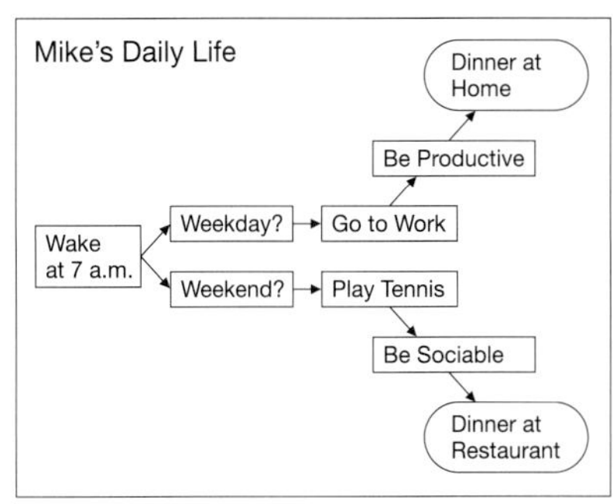

4. ______________________

5. ______________________

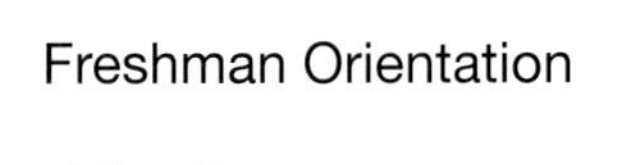

Freshman Orientation
✓ Greetings
✓ Enrollment Procedures
✓ Academic Advising
✓ Campus Tour
✓ Welcome Party

6. ______________________

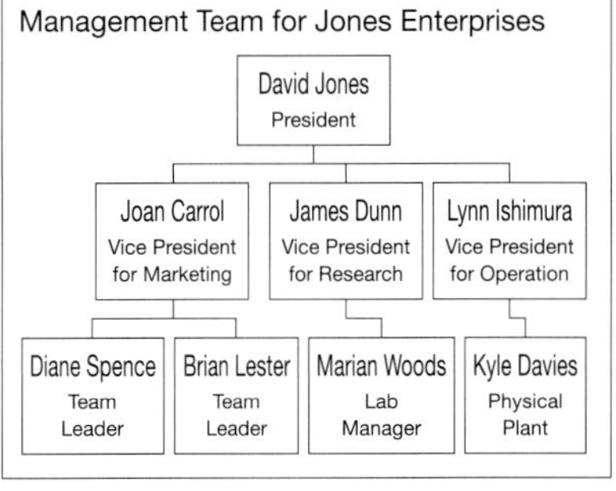

7. ______________________

What type of visual aid would you use for each situation? Write the number from the practice exercise.

____ A presentation on the history of the Samurai sword.
____ An information session for new college students.
____ A description of the process of management decision-making.
____ A discussion of how workers' income has changed in recent years.
____ A board meeting to explain the company's structure to new members.
____ An explanation of the cultural diversity of a college campus.
____ A comparison of salaries for men and women at different times.

Think of more information you might communicate using each type of visual aid.

Outline ______________________

Line Graph ______________________

Bar Graph ______________________

Flow Chart ______________________

Prop ______________________

Pie Chart ______________________

Organizational Chart ______________________

More Practice

Listen to the CD. Which outline visual aid is best for this presentation? Why? What is wrong with the others? Take notes in the space below each visual aid.

James Joyce was an Irish writer who lived most of his life in Europe. His first book was *Dubliners*, a collection of short stories. His second book, *A Portrait of the Artist as a Young Man*, was a semi-autobiographical novel about the development of his artistic consciousness. But his most important book was his third, *Ulysses*, which follows one man through the streets of Dublin on a single day in 1904. It is a great modernist work for which he is most famous. We will talk about his final book, *Finnegans Wake*, at another time.

James Joyce
(1882–1939)

✓ *Dubliners*

✓ *A Portrait of the Artist as a Young Man*

✓ *Ulysses*

James Joyce
Ireland!!!
Dubliners
A Portrait of the Artist as a Young Man
Ulysses
modernism

______ ______ ______ ______

______ ______ ______ ______

Building Your Speech: Supporting Your Speech with Visual Aids

One of the most common uses of visual aids is to clarify abstract statistics. Think back on the presentations you've made for this course. When might a visual aid have helped clarify statistical evidence? What kind would you have made? Think of three examples.

Speech Key 13.3

Visual aids make statistics much more meaningful and memorable.

Type of visual aid: Purpose:

______ ______

______ ______

______ ______

Prepare & Practice

Now choose one from the list above and design a visual aid you could use in a presentation. Conduct further research to find statistical evidence, if necessary. Practice explaining your visual aid to a partner or small group. Critique each other's visual aid and presentation.

Notes on Visual Aid & Presentation

	yes	no		yes	no
Simple?	____	____	Too many graphics?	____	____
Large enough?	____	____	Too many colors?	____	____
Too many fonts?	____	____	Explanation clear?	____	____

What do you like most about this visual aid? ______

Notes for improvement: ______

______

Sound Pronunciation

There are two ways of producing the "l" sound depending on where it occurs in the word.

Light [l] When "l" occurs at the beginning of the word, place your tongue flat to the top of the mouth, touching the front teeth. Voice through the mouth.
▸ lady, line, Larry, letter, lazy

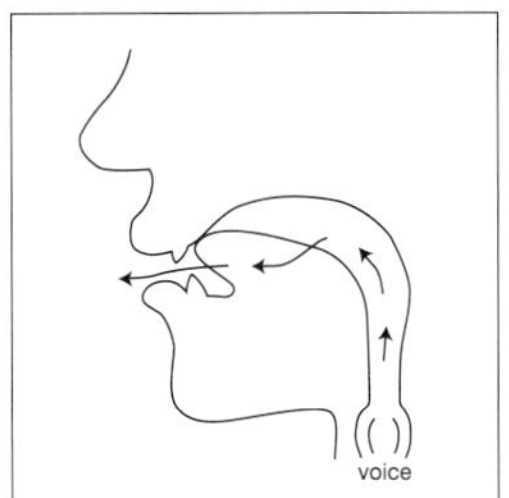

Dark [l] When "l" occurs in the middle or at the end of the word, move your tongue back slightly from the front teeth. Again, voice through the mouth.
▸ fall, taller, whale, curly, believe

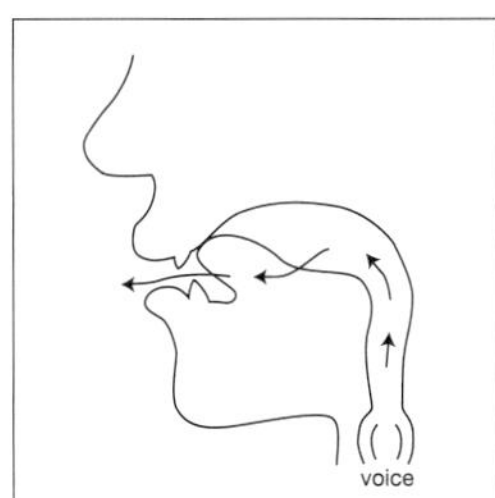

Listen to the CD and repeat the examples. Then make two lists of six more words with "light l" and "dark l" sounds. Practice saying the words with a partner. DL 94 CD 2-26

"Light l" ________ ________ ________
________ ________ ________

"Dark l" ________ ________ ________
________ ________ ________

Stress for Meaning: Predicting Stress

Some two-syllable words may be used as either a noun or a verb. In such cases, the first syllable in nouns is usually stressed, while the second syllable in verbs is stressed.

Noun	Verb
PREsent	preSENT
CONduct	conDUCT
REcord	reCORD
SUSpect	susPECT
DEsert	deSERT

Compound nouns are usually stressed on the first word or syllable.

Compound Nouns	
AIRplane	STOPlight
SOFTware	CREDIT card
CLASSroom	DEADline
BUS station	NEWSpaper

Listen to the CD and repeat. With a partner, make a list of other compound nouns and words that can be used as either nouns or verbs. Practice pronunciation. DL 95 CD 2-27

Compound Nouns

____

____

Nouns/Verbs

____

____

Grammar Review: Modals for Logical Conclusions, Probability, Possibility

We interpret statistics to support our claims, but we can seldom make absolute statements. Therefore, we use modals to express the degree of certainty we feel about the conclusions we draw.

Speech Key 13.4

Don't overstate your claims. Qualify them carefully. The audience will respect your honesty.

Meaning	Past Form	Present/Future	Examples
Logical Conclusion The evidence is very strong, so we speak with near certainty.	*must have* + past participle	*must* + simple present	It's sunny, but the streets are wet. It must have rained earlier. He is getting married soon. He must be excited.
Probability The evidence suggests that our conclusion is likely, but less certain.	*should have* + past participle	*should* + simple present	His plane departed two hours ago. He should have arrived by now. We are winning by 10 points with only one minute left to play. We should win this game.
Possibility The evidence suggests that there is a reasonable chance, but we cannot speak with certainty.	*may/might/could have* + past participle	*may/might/could* + simple present	Where's Bob? I don't know. He might have overslept. Chicago is 11 hours behind Tokyo. You may suffer from jet lag when you arrive.

* You may add stress to the modal to emphasize the degree of certainty.

Write a sentence to express your interpretation and degree of certainty about the following statements.

1. Ninety-eight percent of the people who saw "Jaws" reported having nightmares afterwards.

   ______________________________.

2. Nine out of the ten women Joe has dated have blonde hair.

   ______________________________.

3. Fifty-eight percent of people who regularly eat fast food are overweight.

   ______________________________.

4. The New York Yankees spent $200 million to get the most talented players in baseball.

   ______________________________.

Compare your answers with a partner. Then listen to the CD and check. DL 96 CD 2-28
Notice where stress is placed for emphasis.

Unit 14

Picture This!

Warm-Up

Do you know these famous quotations? Do you know who said them? Match the quotations with the people.

1. "I never let my schooling interfere with my education."
2. "An eye for an eye makes the whole world blind."
3. "Great spirits have always encountered opposition from mediocre minds."

____ Albert Einstein ____ Mark Twain ____ Mahatma Gandhi

Discuss each quotation. What do they mean? What do you know about the people who said them? Which are most inspiring to you? Why?

Appeals II: Appealing to Emotion

A persuasive speech appeals to both the mind and the heart. Your reasons and evidence will appeal to the mind; use emotion to appeal to the heart.

Speech Key 14.1

Don't overdo it! Too much emotion may be seen as manipulative, and it may damage your credibility.

Why Use Emotional Appeals?

* To show your audience you care about the topic.
* To demonstrate importance or urgency.
* To generate excitement or sympathy.
* To supplement appeals to reason and the heart.

Be careful! Emotional appeals are easily misused. The evidence you present and your strong character should drive your speech. Overuse of emotional appeals is manipulative.

How to Appeal to Emotion

* Add stress to key words.
* Increase volume for important phrases.
* Alter the pace to suggest urgency.
* Use tone to show your attitude toward the topic.
* Choose words with emotional impact.

Practice

How would you say the following statements with the appropriate emotion? Where should you add stress or increase volume? Where would you change pace?

1. The Chicago Cubs shocked the world by winning the World Series!
2. After a long, painful fight, cancer claimed the young man's life.
3. My father was absolutely furious when I wrecked the car.

DL 97 CD 2-29
Now listen to the CD and practice again.

Practice

Listen to the CD. You will hear excerpts from different presentations. DL 98 CD 2-30
How does the speaker create emotion? Check (✓) all that apply.

1. ____ volume ____ pace ____ stress ____ tone ____ diction ____ active voice
2. ____ volume ____ pace ____ stress ____ tone ____ diction ____ active voice
3. ____ volume ____ pace ____ stress ____ tone ____ diction ____ active voice
4. ____ volume ____ pace ____ stress ____ tone ____ diction ____ active voice

Visual Aids II: Using Visual Aids

In Unit 13, you learned how to create visual aids to support your presentation. But you must also use them properly. First, you must choose the proper medium. Then practice using them following a few simple rules.

Visual Aid Media

posters flip charts whiteboards chalkboards transparencies slides video handouts

How to Use Visual Aids During a Presentation

1. Introduce the visual aid. Tell your audience what kind of visual aid it is and what kind of information it contains.
2. Explain the visual aid. Tell your audience how to read it (if necessary) and where to find information on it.
3. Highlight the key points of information contained in the visual aid. Make sure the audience understands the information that supports your claims.

Common Errors

* Reading your visual aids. Your audience knows how to read. Just highlight the key points.
* Facing the visual aid and turning away from the audience.
* Relying too much on visual aids. They should support your presentation rather than drive it.
* Forgetting to check equipment before the presentation.

Practice

Read the following statements. Write "I" if the purpose is to introduce a visual aid, "E" to explain, or "H" to highlight specific information.

Speech Key 14.2

Visual aids should support, not drive, your presentation. Don't let them become the focus of attention.

____ As you can see, home sales increased by 50% over the previous year.
____ Please take a look at this pie chart. It shows student enrollment by race.
____ On the vertical axis, you can read the year. On the horizontal axis is the number of houses sold.
____ This line graph shows the trend in consumer confidence and interest rates over time.
____ By following the lines, you can see that lower confidence coincides with higher interest rates.
____ The blue line shows interest rates, and the red line shows consumer confidence.

Compare your answers with a partner.

Practice

Look at the visual aids below. Write sentences to introduce and explain each one and to highlight key information. Work with a partner. Then listen to the CD and compare your answers.

1.

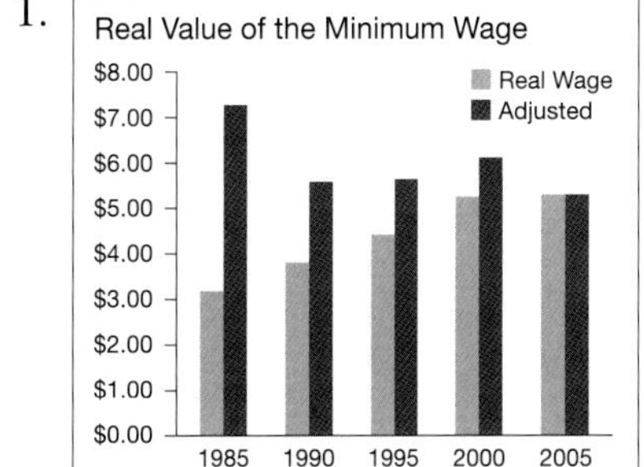

Introduce ____________________
Explain ____________________
Highlight ____________________

2.

Cost of Living
Percent Change (since 1995)
50%
40%
30%
20%
10%
0%
−10%
−20%
Housing
Health Care
Child Care
Minimum Wage

Introduce ____________________
Explain ____________________
Highlight ____________________

3.

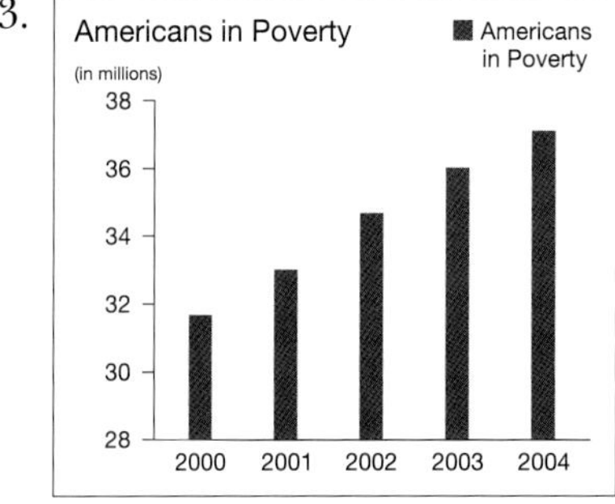

Introduce ____________________
Explain ____________________
Highlight ____________________

Use the blank space to create your own visual aid. Then work in small groups to practice introducing, explaining, and highlighting key information.

Introduce ____________________
Explain ____________________
Highlight ____________________

Building Your Speech: Using Quotations

Quotations can have a dramatic effect on your audience, making your presentation easier to understand and remember. Quotations from experts may also be used as evidence to support your position.

Speech Key 1.3

Quotations are used to add credibility to your speech while making key points clearer and easy to remember.

Use a Quotation to...

...introduce a topic.
...emphasize a key point.
...increase credibility with evidence from an expert.
...give final impact to your presentation.

Who and What to Quote?

Experts with special knowledge of your subject. This type of quotation may also be used as evidence. They may or may not be famous. Always use their names.
Celebrities whom your audience is likely to know and respect. It may be an entertainer, politician, artist, or any public figure.
Friends and family. Unless they are famous, don't use their names.
Proverbs. A proverb is a well-known phrase that offers advice or wisdom. The author is usually unknown.

Match the quotation to the idea it supports.

Quotation

1. "I never let my schooling interfere with my education."
2. "Look before you leap."
3. "Walk softly but carry a big stick."

Idea

a. Think carefully before making a decision.
b. Don't make trouble, but be prepared for it.
c. Experience is an important part of learning.

Now find two more quotations or proverbs. Write them down, then discuss their meaning in a small group.

1. ______________________ 2. ______________________

Prepare & Practice

Your task is to research a controversial topic and prepare a speech based on the following guidelines:

Speech Guidelines

Purpose: Persuade your audience that a problem is serious.

* Create and use at least one visual aid to support your ideas.
* Use emotional appeals to demonstrate urgency.
* Use at least two quotations. One should leave an impression on your audience; one should be evidence from an expert source.

Possible Topics

Famine in Africa
Depression
AIDS
Anorexia Nervosa
Child Abuse
Passive Smoking
Pollution
Youth Violence

Sound Pronunciation

Like "l," the pronunciation of "r" changes depending on its position in a word.

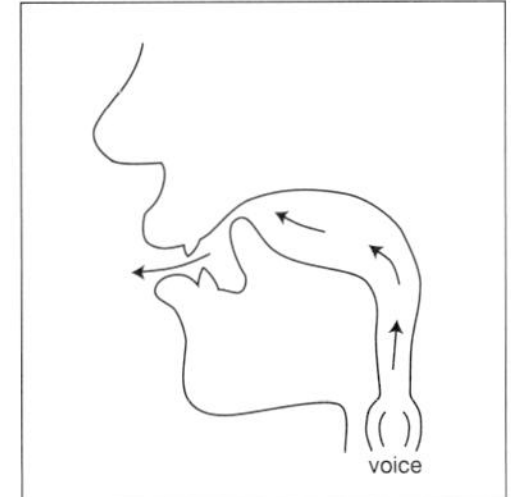

When "r" comes before a vowel, the tip of the tongue goes up, but it doesn't touch the top of the mouth. Place the sides of the tongue to your back teeth.

▶ road, wrong, wrinkle, round, grass, read

The "r" is silent when it comes before a consonant.
Examples: depart, sure, storm, earlier, worse, upstairs, dear, four, later, order

Review pronunciation of light and dark "l" in Unit 13. DL 100 CD 2-32
Then, listen to the CD and repeat the following pairs.

lot/rot bowling/boring climb/crime free/flee law/raw belly/berry
limb/rim light/right late/rate lie/rye rile/Lyle spoil/spore

Practice: Tongue Twisters

The following exercises will help you master the different between "r" and "l."
First, practice repeating these nonsense words many times: luri, liru, luri, liru.

Now listen to the CD and repeat the following words. DL 101 CD 2-33

rural lure rile rule really silly serious leer fury feel leaf roar

Now listen to the CD and practice the following tongue-twisters. DL 102 CD 2-34

1. Laurie and Lawrence rarely lull their really rural relatives with ridiculous lyrics.
2. Crimes and climbs are carefully cleared by careless clowns.
3. Barry's belly is really leery of rare lightly roasted leaves.

Grammar Review: Reported Speech

When using the ideas of others, quote the words directly or report them.

Direct Quotations	Reported Speech
Put the exact words of the original speaker between quotation marks.	1. Go back in tense (i.e., *present* to *past*). 2. Change the pronoun (i.e., *I* to *he/she*). 3. Use *that* to signal reported speech. 4. Drop the quotation marks.
My friend said, "I'm going to visit my grandfather."	My friend said that he was going to visit his grandfather.

* Famous quotations are not changed to reported speech.

Change the following direct quotations into reported speech.

1. The teacher told us, "You will fail the test if you don't study."

   ______________________________.

2. My mother said, "If you work hard, you will always succeed."

   ______________________________.

3. My stern father said, "You can't have any pudding if you don't eat your meat."

   ______________________________.

Change the following reported speech into direct quotations.

1. My boss said that if I didn't perform better, he would fire me.

   ______________________________.

2. The policeman said that I would get a ticket if I didn't slow down.

   ______________________________.

3. The politician said that he would keep all of his promises to us.

   ______________________________.

Compare your answers with a partner. Then listen to the CD and check. DL 103 CD 2-35

Unit 15 Common Ground

Warm-Up

Read about the following disputes. In a small group, discuss how you would resolve each one.

1. Tony Bartolo is a baseball player. Last year, he hit 44 home runs and had a .316 batting average. He wants a new contract worth $18 million per year. The team has offered him $10 million.
2. David, a high school senior, wants to stay out all night with his friends on Graduation Night. His parents told him that he must be home by 12:30 a.m.

How would you resolve these conflicts?

Research Skills I: Finding Information

A key to solving any problem is to be well-informed. You need information to understand a problem and to support your ideas. How will you find the information? Computers have made research easier and faster. You can even work from home to get the most current information available.

> **Speech Key 15.1**
>
> You can't know everything! However, by keeping an open mind and conducting thorough research, you can be well-informed.

Steps for Conducting Research

1. Choose a topic. A good topic is interesting and meets the requirements of the assignment.
2. Read general information. Turn to an encyclopedia or textbook to gain a basic understanding of your topic.
3. Write research questions. What questions do you want to answer? This helps narrow your research.
4. Identify key words. What are the important ideas in your research question? What are the related ideas? Make a list of nouns and synonyms.
5. Search. Use your keywords to look for information in library catalogs, periodical indexes, and the web.
6. Access. Get copies and begin reading.
7. Evaluate. Determine if the information is good and useful. (More on this key skill in Unit 16.)

Computer Research Tools

Databases

* Library catalogs. Most libraries can be accessed online.
* Periodical indexes. Keyword searches can locate the most recent articles on your topic.

Web Search Tools

* Search engines. For recent and specific information.
* Directories. Selective listings of the most relevant information. Browse by category.

Practice

Bob must make a presentation on Global Warming. Put his research plan in order from step 1 to 7.

____ Bob uses his keywords to search online periodical indexes and web directories.

____ Bob decides on a research question: How much greenhouse gases are produced by cars in different countries?

_1_ Bob is given this topic: Global Warming.

____ Bob downloads several articles and reads them.

____ Bob goes to www.wikipedia.com to get some general information about global warming.

____ Bob writes a list of keywords: greenhouse gas, automobile emissions, emissions by country.

Check your answers with a partner.

Choose one of the following topics and make a research plan. Go to the library and find at least two articles to help answer the research question you selected. Work with a partner. Report your results to the class.

Topics: Euthanasia Juvenile Delinquency Obesity Domestic Violence

Practice

Listen to the CD. You will hear a conversation between Bob and a librarian. Read the statements, then circle "T" for true or "F" for false.

DL 104 

The librarian helps Bob identify key words.	T/F
Bob has used the online catalog many times before.	T/F
The librarian shows Bob how to search for articles.	T/F
Bob can print articles, but he can't download them.	T/F
It costs 15 cents to print each page.	T/F
Bob downloads three articles related to his topic.	T/F

Compare your answers with a partner. Then listen again and check.

Mediation

The purpose of a mediation presentation is to bring opposing sides of a dispute together, to find the common ground between them, and help them reach a compromise.

Speech Key 15.2

Effective mediators earn the trust of both sides by remaining impartial and establishing trust.

Conditions for Mediation

* Both sides must have valid claims.
* Most of the people on both sides must be willing to compromise.
* The mediator must be impartial.

Preliminary Questions for Mediation

* What is disputed? What is its history?
* Who are the opposing sides? What do they value? How does the dispute affect them?
* How does each side view the dispute?
* What do the two sides have in common?

Building Your Speech: Structure for a Mediation Presentation

The following structure is suggested for mediation presentations.

I. Introduction: What is the Dispute?
   A. The history of the dispute
   B. The current situation
II. Describe Side 1
   A. Who are they?
   B. What is important to them?
   C. What is their view of the dispute?
III. Describe Side 2
   A. Who are they?
   B. What is important to them?
   C. What is their view of the dispute?
IV. Summarize the Differences

Strategies for Mediation

* Appeal to the hearts and minds of both parties. Remain impartial and make sure you are well-informed.
* Appeal using reason. Use the information you've gathered to support your ideas.
* Avoid over-emotional appeals. Your job is to reduce passions on both sides and find common ground.

V. Identify Common Concerns
VI. Propose a Solution
VII. Conclusion

Practice

Listen to the CD. You will hear a mediation presentation on a very controversial topic in the US Answer the following questions. online video DL 105 CD 2-37

1. What is the topic of the dispute? ______
2. When did the dispute begin? Why? ______
3. What is the current situation? ______
4. What term is used to describe one side? ______
5. What is important to them? ______
6. How do they view the dispute? ______
7. What term is used to describe the other side? ______
8. What is important to them? ______
9. How do they view the dispute? ______
10. What is the main difference? ______
11. What are the common concerns? ______
12. What solution is proposed? ______
13. What point is made in conclusion? ______

Compare your answers with a partner. Then listen again and check.

Caution!

In most controversial disputes, there are extremists on both sides who will not compromise. They are not your audience. Try to communicate with reasonable, open-minded people in the middle who are willing to work together to find solutions.

Prepare

Prepare a mediation presentation to help opposing sides to find common ground. Start by brainstorming some possible topics.

Possible Topics for Mediation

____

____

____

____

____

Step 1. Choose your topic: ________________

Step 2. Get some general information about your topic.

Step 3. Write some questions to guide your research.

____

____

____

Step 4. Identify some key words to guide your search for information.

________________ ________________

________________ ________________

Step 5. Go to the library and search for information.

Step 6. Gather the information you need and begin reading.

Once you have gathered information and learned about your topic, outline a mediation presentation.

I. Introduction: The Dispute ____________________

History ____________________

Current situation ____________________

II. Side 1. Who are they? ____________________

What is important to them? ____________________

How do they view the dispute? ____________________

III. Side 2. Who are they? ____________________

What is important to them? ____________________

How do they view the dispute? ____________________

IV. Summarize their differences ____________________

V. Identify common concerns ____________________

VI. Propose a solution ____________________

VII. Conclusion ____________________

Now develop your presentation. Design and use visual aids, if they will help support your points.

Practice

Work with a partner and practice your presentation.
Use the following questions to help your partner improve.

1. Is the dispute clearly explained? What questions do you have about the dispute?
2. Are both sides of the dispute explained? What else would you like to know about either side?
3. Does the speaker identify common ground? Do you think the majority of people on both sides will agree?
4. Do you think the proposed solution will satisfy many people on both sides?
5. Does the speaker establish character and remain impartial?
6. What is the greatest strength of your partner's presentation? The greatest weakness?

Sound Pronunciation

The "b" sound is formed by holding your lips together and pushing air outward as the sound is made while opening the lips.

▶ bowl, beer, boom, bale, barber, beautiful, bin

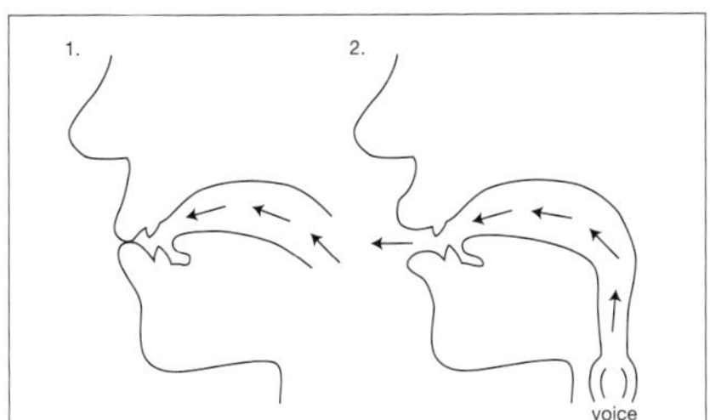

The "v" sound is formed by placing the upper front teeth on the lower lip and pushing air outward as the sound is made.

▶ view, veil, very, Vinny, van, violate, vocal

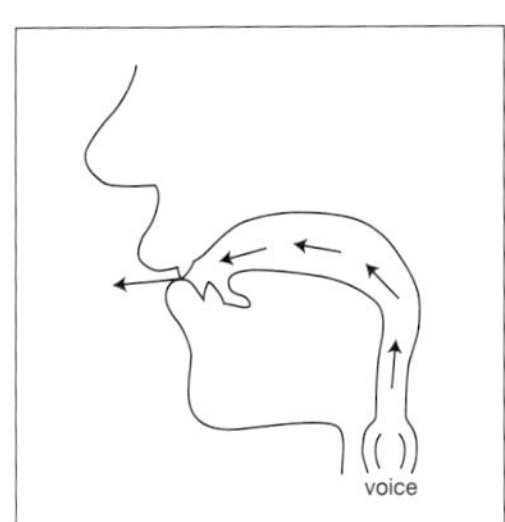

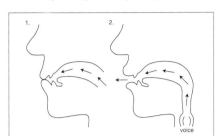

Listen to the CD and repeat. DL 106 CD 2-38

Listen to the CD and circle the words you hear. DL 107 CD 2-39
Then practice pronouncing both words in each pair.

1. very/berry 2. base/vase 3. bail/veil 4. bet/vet
5. vote/boat 6. ban/van 7. bolt/volt 8. best/vest

Listen to the CD and write down the words you hear. DL 108 CD 2-40

1. ____________________ 2. ____________________
3. ____________________ 4. ____________________

Compare your answers with a partner. Then listen again and repeat.

Stress Practice: Changing Stress in Changing Word Forms

As the form of a word may change to create new words, so changes the stress. Luckily, the stress patterns are often predictable.

Listen to the CD and repeat the following words. Mark the stress for each word. DL 109 CD 2-41

1. final	finality	finalize	finalization
2. neutral	neutrality	neutralize	neutralization
3. equal	equality	equalize	equalization
4. mediate	mediator	mediation	

Grammar Review: Word Formation

You can expand your vocabulary quickly if you understand word formation. By changing the endings of words, you can change a verb into a noun, a noun into an adjective, and so on. Let's practice some of the most common word endings.

Common Noun Endings	Common Adjective Endings	Common Adjective Endings
~ance/ence. Ex. attendance	~y. Ex. hairy, sunny, funny	~ed. Ex. excited, interested
~ment. Ex. entertainment	~ous. Ex. tremendous	~ing. Ex. exciting, interesting
~ation. Ex. presentation	~ary. Ex. secondary	
~er/or. Ex. professor, teacher	~ish. Ex. foolish, childish	
~sion. Ex. extension	~ic. Ex. scientific, artistic	
~tion. Ex. education	~ful/less. Ex. faithful, fearless	

* Note. As an adjective, the past participle *~ed* is used to describe people's feelings or condition. The present participle *~ing* is used to describe the condition of an object or idea.

Fill in the chart with other forms of the words given.

Verb	Noun	Adjective
irritate		
	permission	
		related
require		
	actor	
		preferred
imagine		
	difference	

Check your answers with a partner. Then listen to the CD and repeat. DL 110 CD 2-42

Unit 16

In Conclusion...

Warm-Up

Put a check (✓) in the first column of blanks next to the statements you might hear in the conclusion of a presentation.

____ ____ Thank you for your time.
____ ____ Let me recap the main points.
____ ____ I'd be happy to answer your questions now.
____ ____ In this short time, I have tried to explain to you...
____ ____ I'd like to wrap things up with a quotation from...
____ ____ I hope you've found this presentation informative.
____ ____ It's been a pleasure speaking with you today.

Now listen to the CD. Which statements do you hear? Number them from 1 to 5 in the second column of blanks.

Research Skills II: Evaluating Information

You have conducted research, but how do you know if you have good information? You must evaluate the information to determine if it is good support for your ideas.

Speech Key 16.1

Evaluate all information you plan to use. Protect your credibility and strengthen your ideas.

Critical Questions for Evaluating Information

1. Is the information current? Is more recent information available?
2. What is the coverage of the information? Does it answer your research questions?
3. Is the source of information authoritative? Who wrote it?

Assign each member of your group one of the following questions. Go to the library, find the answers and report them to your group.

Where would you look for current information about the economy in your country?
Where would you look for information about changes in the value of the US dollar over the last five years?
What sources of economic information do you think are authoritative?

Practice

Practice asking questions to evaluate sources.

1. The importance of currency is different for each of the following presentation topics. Rate them from 1 (most important) to 4 (least important).
   ____ The severity of global warming
   ____ The growth of Boston in the 17th century
   ____ How to build an energy-efficient home
   ____ Cloning

2. Put a check (✓) next to the piece of information which, if true, would provide the best supporting detail for the idea that "Automobiles are a primary source of greenhouse gasses."
   ____ Greenhouse gas emissions have increased by 25% since 1900.
   ____ Automobiles add 22 million tons, or 15%, of annual greenhouse gasses to the atmosphere.
   ____ Automobiles create greenhouse gasses.
   ____ Americans drive more miles annually than any other people.

3. Which source of information would likely be most authoritative and unbiased for the information in question 2?
   ____ The American Petroleum Producers Association
   ____ The Anti-Technology Society
   ____ A Cornell University graduate student who majored in literature.
   ____ A commission of Nobel Prize-winning scientists

Compare and discuss your answers.

Practice

Listen to the CD. You will hear a presentation about changes in the value of the US dollar over the past five years. Answer the questions. DL 112 CD 2-44

1. What statistic does the speaker mention?

   ____

2. What is the source of the statistic?

   ____

3. What point does the statistic support?

   ____

4. Do you think the statistic is good evidence? Why or why not?

   ____

Discuss your answers in a small group.

Building Your Speech: Conclusions

The conclusion is your last chance to make an impression on your audience. By planning it carefully and practicing, you can make your conclusion a very powerful part of your presentation.

Functions of the Conclusion

1. Signals the end of the presentation. Remember, you must always guide your audience. Make it clear that the presentation is coming to an end.
2. Reinforces the main idea. This is your last chance to make sure your audience understands you.

How to Reinforce the Main Idea

✓ Summarize the presentation. Restate the main points so they are the last words your audience hears.

✓ Use a quotation if you can find a brief and memorable one that suits your main points. Your audience is likely to remember it.

✓ Refer to the introduction. At the beginning of your presentation, you explained the purpose and told the audience what to expect.

✓ Use your final comments to ensure that your audience understands important points.

How to Signal the End of Your Presentation

Use signal expressions:

* In conclusion…
* In closing…
* Let me end by saying…

Change your delivery style:

* Insert a pause.
* Alter the pace, tone, or volume.

Speech Key 16.2

The conclusion is your final interaction with the audience. Try to make a strong, lasting impression.

Practice

Listen to the CD. Focus on the conclusion of the presentation and answer the questions.   

1. How does the speaker signal the end of the presentation?

____

2. What main idea is reinforced?

____

3. What reason for supporting the policy is given?

____

Prepare: Policy Presentation

In a policy presentation, questions of whether or not a specific course of action should be taken are addressed. The possible topics for such a presentation are almost endless. We have discussions on policy every day—about important national or international topics such as what to do about famine in Africa, or local and personal topics, such as what kind of food to feed a young child. In a policy presentation, you can use all of the skills you have studied in this course so far to persuade your audience.

Prepare a short presentation based on the following guidelines.

1. Persuade your classmates to adopt a particular policy or take a specific course of action. You may choose any topic. See the examples on the right for ideas.
2. Find, evaluate, and use at least 3 sources of information to support your idea.
3. Create and use at least 2 visual aids.
4. Signal the conclusion and reinforce the main idea.

Example Policy Proposals

1. Smoking should be banned in all public places.
2. You should not drink more than two cups of coffee per day.
3. English should be taught in all public elementary schools.
4. Children should be required to wear a helmet when cycling.

Practice

Once you have prepared your policy presentation, practice with a partner. Help your partner improve his or her speech by evaluating the following features.

Evaluating Visual Aids

	yes	no
Creation		
Simple?	____	____
Large enough?	____	____
Appropriate graphics?	____	____
Overused?	____	____
Usage/Implementation		
Introduced?	____	____
Explained?	____	____
Points highlighted?	____	____

Evaluating Sources

For each piece of information, ask the following:

	yes	no
Is it current?	____	____
Is coverage sufficient?	____	____
Is the source authoritative?	____	____
Is more evidence needed?	____	____

Evaluating the Conclusion

How is the conclusion signaled?

____

____

Suggest improvements: __________

____

How are the main points reinforced?

____

____

Suggest improvements: __________

____

Perform

Present your policy presentation to your class. Afterwards, take a vote to see if you persuaded your classmates to adopt your idea.

Sound Pronunciation

In Unit 15 we learned the difference between the "b" and "v" sounds. The "w" sound is similar. To make the "w" sound, first make the ʌ, then purse your lips and push air through your lips as you open your mouth.

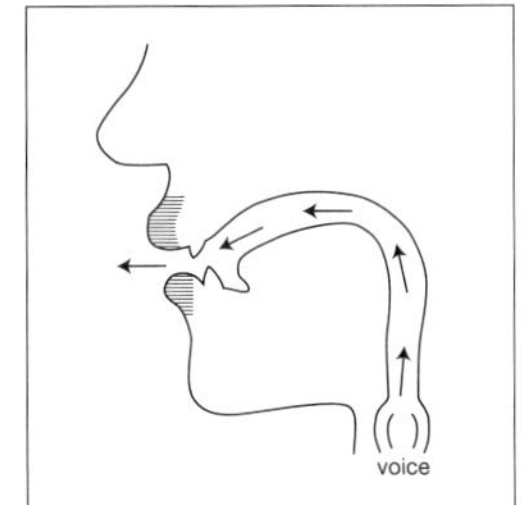

▶ wide, wacky, wonder, Wayne, win, wow, where

Listen to the CD and repeat. DL 114 CD 2-46

Listen to the CD and circle the words you hear. DL 115 CD 2-47

whale/veil west/vest vile/while vein/wane wary/very vine/wine

Check your answers with a partner, then listen again.

Listen to the CD and practice the tongue twisters. DL 116 CD 2-48

How much wood would a woodchuck chuck if a woodchuck could chuck wood?
Very wonderful Vermont winter weather winds its way westward.

Stress for Meaning: Rhetorical Questions

Rhetorical questions—or questions asked to produce an effect, without expectation that they will be answered—may be used to create a conversational tone, establish rapport, and guide the audience by focusing attention on information to come.

Listen to the CD. Underline the words or syllables that receive heavy stress. DL 117 CD 2-49
The first one is done for you.

1. So how serious is the problem? It's very serious. Let me explain...
2. How did the problem become so serious? There is plenty of blame to go around.
3. What can you do to help? You can start by learning about the problem.
4. So where does the solution lie? It lies within you.
5. How certain am I that we can solve this problem? I have complete confidence. Here's why...

Compare your answers with a partner. Then listen again and repeat. Work with a partner and write two more rhetorical questions. Share them with the class.

____

____

____

____

____

Grammar Review: Expressing Necessity or Prohibition

To make very strong policy statements, use expressions of necessity or prohibition.

Necessity	Prohibition
must + simple verb We must protect children from harm. You must pass the test to graduate.	*must not* + simple verb You must not smoke in public areas. We must not ignore this problem.
have/has to + simple verb We have to consider all possible solutions. I have to submit the report by Friday.	
need/needs to + simple verb We need to work together to find a solution. I need to renew my passport soon.	

* Note: The negative expressions, *do not have to,* and *do not need to* are not used to express prohibition. Instead, they are used to express lack of necessity. Ex. You don't have to take this course if you don't want to.

** Note: You can create a sense of urgency by adding stress. Ex. We **must** solve this problem.

Write sentences to express necessity and prohibition in response to each statement.

1. Bob and Jane want to get married, but Bob is still married to another woman.
   Prohibition: ______________________________
   Necessity: ______________________________
2. Jeremy plans to study abroad next year, but he doesn't have a passport.
   Prohibition: ______________________________
   Necessity: ______________________________
3. Helen's doctor says that if she doesn't improve her health, she could become very sick.
   Prohibition: ______________________________
   Necessity: ______________________________

Compare your answers with a partner. Then listen to the model answers on the CD. DL 118 CD 2-50

Unit 17

Any Questions?

Warm-Up

Put a check (✓) next to the situations you have experienced.

Have you ever…

____ had a job interview?
____ tried to persuade a friend to join you for dinner?
____ explained to a teacher why you were late for class?
____ shared your thoughts in a group discussion?
____ given advice to a friend?

Discuss your answers in a small group. How did you handle each situation?

Research Skills III: Avoiding Plagiarism

Plagiarism—presenting another person's ideas or words as your own—is not accepted in most academic or professional communities around the world. In a formal presentation, you could lose the trust and respect of your audience.

The most effective way to avoid plagiarism is to explicitly and accurately cite each source.

Speech Key 17.1

Intentional plagiarism makes you appear dishonest. Unintentional plagiarism makes you appear careless. Both damage credibility.

Types of Plagiarism

Intentional: A writer or speaker knowingly presents the ideas of others as his or her own. Unintentional: A writer or speaker fails to credit the original source—either through forgetfulness or inaccuracy.

How to Cite Your Sources

1. Refer to the source during your presentation.
   Ex. According to…
   In a recent study by…
2. Create a bibliography so that audience members can find the original source. You can share the bibliography in two ways:
   * If you are using slides, put the bibliography on the final slide.
   * Put the bibliography on a handout.

Referring to the Source

X Nearly 25% of all teenage boys smoke.

✓ According to the National Institute for Health, nearly 25% of all teenage boys smoke.

Practice

Look at the following sample bibliography entry. Label the elements with the terms below.

______ ______ ______

Smith, D. (2004). "Recent trends in reading research."
The Journal of Educational Psychology, 90(2), 115-146.

______ ______ ______

page numbers title of article author's name
volume and issue numbers title of journal
year of publication

American Psychological Association (APA) format is a common and general reference format. Use the format appropriate for your field.

Practice

Create a bibliography of sources for one of the presentations you made for this course. For more information on citing sources, visit Purdue University's online writing resource center at: http://owlenglish.purdue.edu/owl/resource/560/01/

Basic Guidelines for Bibliographies (APA)

1. List entries alphabetically by the author's last name.
2. Use only initials for first and middle names.
3. Put the year of publication in parentheses after the author's name.
4. Capitalize the first letter of the first word of article and book titles.
5. Capitalize the first letter of each main word in journal titles.
6. Use italics for book titles and journal names.
7. When citing internet sources, include the URL.

Speech Key 17.2

Protect yourself from plagiarism with a clear and accurate bibliography.

Compare your bibliography with a partner.

Building Your Speech: Preparing for Questions

Your audience will usually have questions for you at the end of your presentation. Be prepared for them. Look back at one of the presentations you've made for this course. Write at least three questions you think your audience might have. Then write model answers to the questions. Practice delivery in a small group.

Preparing for Questions

Anticipate questions. Think about your audience. What key points might they want to know more about?
Write model answers. Once you have identified possible questions, prepare your answers.
Practice delivering answers. Just like every other part of your speech, you should practice many times.

Building Your Speech: Answering Questions

Now that you have prepared for answering questions, you are more likely to feel confident when you are asked real questions. The following hints will help you answer questions more effectively.

Answering Questions

✓ **Set the rules.** In your introduction, tell your audience if it is okay to ask questions during the presentation or if they should wait until the end.

✓ **Be positive.** There is no such thing as a bad question. A question gives you the chance to expand upon or reinforce a point. Welcome all questions.

✓ **Listen!** The most successful leaders are also good listeners. Listen to understand and empathize with the audience.

✓ **Answer the entire audience.** The Q & A session should not be a dialogue between you and the questioner. The audience still exists. One technique is to repeat the question. This confirms that you heard the question correctly while including the entire audience in the discussion.

✓ **Stay focused.** There will usually be only a few minutes for questions. Long, rambling answers will take too long and bore everyone. Answer the question fully, but as quickly as possible, then move on to the next question.

Practice

Listen to the CD. You will hear a Question and Answer session from two different presentations. Take notes on each presentation. Then put a check (✓) next to the best one. Why was it better? Why was the other one worse?

DL 119 CD 2-51

Evaluating the Q & A

Session A ____

Notes: ______________________________

____

____

____

Evaluating the Q & A

Session B ____

Notes: ______________________________

____

____

____

Discuss your answers in a small group. Then listen again and check.

Practice

Take just 5 minutes to prepare a very short, informal presentation on any topic that interests you. Then take two more minutes to write down one or two questions your classmates might ask about your presentation. Think about how you will answer them. Finally, perform your presentation. Take at least two questions from your audience and answer them, keeping in mind the principles outlined above.

Impromptu Speaking

You may someday be asked to make an impromptu presentation—a short speech with little or no time to prepare. For many people, this causes great anxiety. But you should be relieved to know that you have already made many impromptu speeches in your life. So take a deep breath, take the following steps, and proceed with confidence!

The best way to develop confidence for impromptu speaking is to practice. The more often you give an impromptu speech, the more skilled you will become. With practice, you will learn to organize your thoughts quickly and express them clearly.

Steps for Impromptu Speaking

1. **Be Calm!** You already have the skills you need to be successful. Usually, the audience knows that you are speaking with little preparation. Therefore, their expectations are lower than they might be for a formal presentation.
2. **Listen!** You may be asked to respond to other people's comments. Take notes as you listen, think of how you might respond.
3. **Sketch an outline**, if you have time. This needn't be detailed or developed. It is intended to help you stay focused and cover all of the points you wish to discuss. A few key words may be sufficient.
4. **Structure your comments:**
   a. State the topic or point to which you are responding.
   b. State your position or point.
   c. Explain your position with details or evidence.
   d. Summarize your point.

Practice

Form a group of five or six students. Each student should write a topic on a small sheet of paper. Any topic is okay, but it should be something that doesn't require specific knowledge, so anyone can speak about it. Fold all the papers in half and gather them together. The first speaker should draw a topic and take five minutes to prepare an impromptu speech on it. As the first student begins to speak, the next student should draw a topic and prepare until the first student's impromptu presentation is finished and then give his or her speech. Repeat these steps until all group members have made an impromptu presentation. Be prepared to ask a question after each presentation. Complete the chart.

Speaker	Topic	Question	Comments
Yuka Kurose	*college life*	*What do you enjoy most about your college life?*	*She used personal experience to explain her point.*

Sound Pronunciation: Pronouncing New Words

In the course of your research you may come across many new words. In addition to learning their meanings, you must also learn how to pronounce them correctly. Match the words on the left with their written phonetic forms on the right. Then practice pronouncing the words.

1. vaccination	a. indʒíːnjəs
2. chronology	b. zéləs
3. theocratic	c. θéərəpjúːtik
4. ingenious	d. kəmpʌ́lʃən
5. zealous	e. væksənéiʃən
6. compulsion	f. krənɑ́lədʒi
7. therapeutic	g. θiəkrǽtik

Check your answers with a partner and practice pronunciation. DL 120 CD 2-52
Then listen to the CD and repeat in the pauses.

Stress for Meaning

Questions may end with rising or falling pitch, depending on the type of question.

1. *Wh~* questions usually end with falling pitch. Ex. What did you have for lunch?
2. *Yes/No* questions end with rising pitch. Ex. Did you remember to bring your homework?

Mark the following questions with an arrow to show rising or falling intonation.

1. What are you doing this weekend? _____
2. Are you going to graduate this year? _____
3. How long have you been waiting? _____
4. Do you play baseball every weekend? _____

Practice saying the questions with a partner. Then listen to the CD and check. 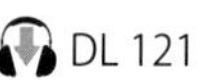 DL 121 CD 2-53

Grammar Review: Articles

By using the articles, *a*, *an*, and *the* correctly, your English will sound more fluent and natural. It takes a lot of practice to master these articles. Here are the basic rules to get you started.

	Definite-countable	Definite-uncountable	Indefinite-countable	Indefinite-uncountable
Singular	The house is lovely.	The coffee is delicious.	I would like to buy a house.	I drink too much coffee.
	The player is happy.	The fruit in my supermarket is always fresh.	A baseball player earns a high salary.	Fruit is my favorite snack.
Plural	The trains are always crowded.		Trains are more efficient than cars.	
			Houses can be very expensive.	

There are three main points to consider when making decisions about articles:

1. Is the noun countable or uncountable?
2. If it is countable, is it singular or plural?
3. Does it have a definite or indefinite meaning? In other words, are you referring to something specific? Or is the meaning more general?

Fill in the blanks with "a," "an," "the," or "X."

1. My sister Laurie has always been ______ excellent singer. When she was ______ teenager, she won ______ talent show.
2. ______ 1927 Yankees are considered by many to be ______ best baseball team in ______ history.
3. I told ______ teacher that ______ homework was eaten by a dog, but he said that I shouldn't make ______ excuses.
4. My brother never drinks ______ coffee at ______ office. Instead, he visits ______ cafe after he finishes ______ work.

Compare your answers with a partner. Then listen to the CD and check. DL 122 CD 2-54

Unit 18 Review

Wrapping Up

Throughout this course, you have learned a wide variety of new skills and strategies, and you have gained experience using them in front of a live audience. You should now have all the tools you need to make dynamic presentations in any situation. Refer to the following steps to help you build presentations in the future.

Step 1: Consider the Context

Start by taking preliminary notes on the context. What are you being asked to talk about? Why? Where will the presentation take place? How much time do you have to prepare? What resources are available for the presentation? How much time will you have?

Preliminary Notes on Context

Step 2: Choose Your Topic

In real life, you may have complete freedom to choose your topic, or it may be chosen for you. At other times, you will have freedom to choose a topic within a specific range. If you have some freedom, begin by brainstorming a list of suitable topics. Then choose one and brainstorm everything you already know or believe about your topic.

Brainstorm a List of Topics

Brainstorm Ideas about Your Topic

Describe your topic. What do you know about it? What is its history? How do you feel about it? How do others feel about it? What do you need to learn about it?

Step 3: Consider Your Purpose

Context, purpose, and topic are inseparable. For example, if you are to give a speech at a friend's wedding, your topic is probably going to be your friend and his or her spouse and your relationship to them, and your thoughts about their wedding. Your purpose is to entertain and inform. Knowing this, you can better proceed to select and organize information to suit your purpose. In this course, you have given presentations for some of the most common purposes. Look at the following chart for examples of the kinds of presentations that are made for different purposes.

Entertain	Inform	Explain	Persuade
Wedding Speech	Self-Introduction	Giving Directions	Problem Solving
Retirement Toast	Talk about Goals or Dreams	How to Do or Make Something	Mediation
Dinner Party Speech	Discuss Current Events	Cause & Effect Comparison/Contrast	Policy Speech

Step 4: Analyze Your Audience

By understanding your audience, you can select information and use strategies to communicate most effectively. Who is your audience? What do they know about the topic? What do they need to know? What are their values? What level of language would be appropriate for this audience? What kind of evidence would be most convincing? What appeals would be effective? Take a few minutes and brainstorm everything you know or believe about your audience.

Brainstorming: Audience Analysis

Step 5: Research Your Topic

Now gather more information about your topic. Use the ideas you brainstormed earlier as a starting point, then take the following steps.

Research Checklist

1. Read general information on your topic.
2. Write research questions.
3. Identify key words.
4. Search for information.
5. Access information.
6. Evaluate information and sources.

Step 6: Organize Your Ideas

Once you have found and evaluated information you can begin to organize it. You might start by clustering ideas to help you decide upon a pattern of organization. When you feel you are ready, begin writing an outline. As you proceed, keep in mind the context, topic, purpose, and audience.

Preliminary Outline

As you write your outline, you may discover that you need more information. Return to the library, if necessary.

Step 7: Write Your Speech

Now write the text of your speech. Use your outline to keep yourself focused, but don't be afraid to make changes if necessary. Keep your audience in mind: What level of language would be most effective for this audience? What types of appeals will be most effective given this audience's values?

Once you have written your first draft, look at it critically to make sure you have achieved your purpose. Then revise your speech accordingly.

Remember to use quotations to make your points stronger and clearer. Refer to sources of information appropriately to avoid plagiarism.

10 Critical Questions

1. Have I introduced myself and my topic in the introduction?
2. Have I told the audience when to ask questions?
3. Is my main idea clearly stated?
4. Have I explained good reasons or supporting ideas in support of the main idea?
5. Is there sufficient support for each point?
6. Is the language clear and appropriate?
7. Do I stay focused on the points I am trying to make?
8. Do I make a strong impression in the conclusion?
9. What is the best part of this draft?
10. What is the weakest part of this draft?

Step 8: Create Visual Aids

Identify the information in your speech that could be made clearer by the use of visual aids. Which ideas are complex or abstract? Which ideas are the most important for your audience? Once you have identified information you wish to present visually, take the following steps.

Steps for Creating Visual Aids

1. Decide which type of visual aid is the most appropriate. (See the list in Unit 13.)
2. Choose a medium. (See the list in Unit 14.)
3. Decide the content and create the visual aid according to the following principles:
   a. Keep it simple.
   b. Make it large enough.
   c. Avoid distractions.
   d. Don't overuse it.

Step 9: Cite Your Sources

It is always necessary to give credit for the information you use. If you are quoting a famous person, referring to his or her name in the speech is sufficient. In most informal presentations, simply referring to the source of the information in your speech will satisfy most members of your audience. However, in more formal presentations in which you draw on research, you should cite every source you used in a bibliography. Your bibliography might be a final slide, or it could be a handout that you give to your audience at the end of the presentation. (Refer to the guidelines in Unit 17.)

Step 10: Practice! Practice! Practice!

Even the best speakers practice delivering their presentations many times before the actual performance. Therefore, it is even more important for the inexperienced presenter to practice.

Reasons to Practice

1. **Practice builds confidence.** The more familiar you are with your speech, the less likely you are to have anxiety over your presentation.
2. **Practice builds fluency.** By repeatedly pronouncing words and using appropriate stress, your English will become more natural and easier to understand.
3. **Practice reduces errors.** With extra practice, you are less likely to forget key points or lose focus as you speak.

Tips for Efficient Practice

1. **Time Yourself.** You will usually have a time limit for your presentation. Make sure you stay within the limit. Revise your presentation for time if necessary.
2. **Always practice aloud.** Use your voice as you actually plan to use it during the presentation. Practice volume, tone, pace, and expression. Practice pronunciation and stress.
3. **Make your practice as real as possible.** If you plan to use visual aids, practice with them. If you will make your presentation behind a podium, practice behind one. If you have access to the actual site where you will make the presentation, practice there so you will be familiar with the surroundings.
4. **Practice in front of an audience.** Ask a friend or colleague to serve as a practice audience. You will get valuable feed back about your presentation. This will also help you anticipate questions.

Step 11: Final Preparations

1. Get a good night's sleep before your presentation.
2. Check your appearance. Make sure your clothes are appropriate for the type of presentation.
3. Arrive early. Check that there are no last-minute schedule or site changes.
4. Check your equipment. Make sure slide projectors and monitors are working properly.
5. Make sure you have enough handouts.
6. Drink some water! Also, make sure there is additional water available during your presentation.
7. Find a quiet place to relax, breathe deeply, and clear your mind of distractions before the presentation begins.

Presentation Checklist

Use the following checklist as a reference to help you prepare for presentations in the future.

Step 1: Consider the Context ____

Step 2: Choose Your Topic ____

Step 3: Consider Your Purpose ____

Step 4: Analyze Your Audience ____

Step 5: Research Your Topic ____

Step 6: Organize Your Information ____

Step 7: Write Your Speech ____

Step 8: Create Visual Aids ____

Step 9: Cite Your Sources ____

Step 10: Practice! Practice! Practice! ____

Step 11: Final Checks ____

Final Words

Preparing for and making presentations is a great opportunity for personal growth and expression. You can expand your own understanding of the world and share that understanding with others. Everyone wins!

Keep this book and refer to it as you are called upon to make presentations throughout your personal life and professional career. We hope it will be of value to you years after the course is over.

Good luck, and have fun!

Key Expressions & Vocabulary

Unit 1

▶ The following expressions may be useful when working in groups or pairs:

What do you think about this topic?

Could you explain?

Fill in the blanks with the words below.

pronunciation	persuade	collaborate	definition	context

1. ________________ (v.) to work together.
2. ________________ (n.) the time, place and circumstances where something happens.
3. ________________ (n.) the sound of a word.
4. ________________ (v.) to convince someone to do or believe something.
5. ________________ (n.) the meaning of a word.

Unit 2

▶ A good speech starts with a greeting:

Ladies and Gentlemen, thank you for your participation today.

Ladies and Gentlemen, it is a pleasure to talk with you today.

Fill in the blanks with the words below.

topics	audience	vowel	purpose	perform

1. ______________ (n.) the subjects you talk about in your speech.
2. ______________ (n.) the people who listen to your speech.
3. ______________ (v.) to make your speech.
4. ______________ (n.) a speech sound made with the letters *a*, *e*, *i*, *o*, *u*, and sometimes *y*.
5. ______________ (n.) reason for doing something.

Unit 3

▶ When introducing someone else, these expressions may be useful:

Today I'd like to talk about a very special person.
My purpose today is to tell you about a person whom I admire greatly.

Fill in the blanks with the words below.

sway	consonants	appearance	delivery	confidence

1. ______________ (v.) to move side to side.
2. ______________ (n.) the way a speech is presented to an audience.
3. ______________ (n.) how someone looks.
4. ______________ (n.) a strong, positive feeling about something or someone.
5. ______________ (n.) speech sounds that are not vowels, for example *b, c, d, f, g, etc.*

Unit 4

▶ Gestures are often used with heavily stressed words for added emphasis:

I've NEVER been to a more interesting city.
SECONDLY, I suggest you take in a ballgame at Wrigley Field.

Fill in the blanks with the words below.

spontaneous	gesture	clustering	brainstorming	excerpt

1. ______________ (n.) a part of a text.
2. ______________ (adj.) not planned.
3. ______________ (n.) a method of generating ideas by listing or free writing.
4. ______________ (n.) non-verbal communication using hands.
5. ______________ (n.) a method of generating and organizing details quickly.

Unit 5

▶ Transitions guide your audience as you move from point to point:

First, let me preview the main points.

In conclusion, let's review some key points from today's discussion.

Fill in the blanks with the words below.

enunciate	transition	conclusion	summary	illustrate

1. ______________ (n.) word or phrase used to move from one topic to another.
2. ______________ (v.) to pronounce fully.
3. ______________ (v.) to clarify words with examples.
4. ______________ (n.) an ending.
5. ______________ (n.) a restatement of the main points.

Unit 6

▶ The following expressions may be used to introduce a past event:

Let me tell you about an important event in my life.

I'd like to share with you a story from my past.

Fill in the blanks with the words below.

situation	diaphragm	project	destroyed	breathe

1. ______________ (n.) muscle used to push air over the vocal chords.
2. ______________ (n.) the time, place, and details of an event.
3. ______________ (v.) to take air in and out of your lungs.
4. ______________ (adj.) useless, dead, or defeated.
5. ______________ (v.) to make louder.

Unit 7

▶ These expressions may be used when introducing current events:

In the news recently...

I'd like to discuss an issue currently in the news.

Fill in the blanks with the words below.

verifiable	pace	relevant	required	declining

1. ______________ (adj.) needed or necessary.
2. ______________ (n.) the speed at which something is done.
3. ______________ (adj.) something that can be proven true.
4. ______________ (adj.) important in relation to a topic or subject; pertinent.
5. ______________ (adj.) going down.

Unit 8

▶ These expressions can be used when describing problems and explaining causes:

I want to tell you about an urgent problem.

I'd like to explain what I believe to be the causes of this phenomenon.

Fill in the blanks with the words below.

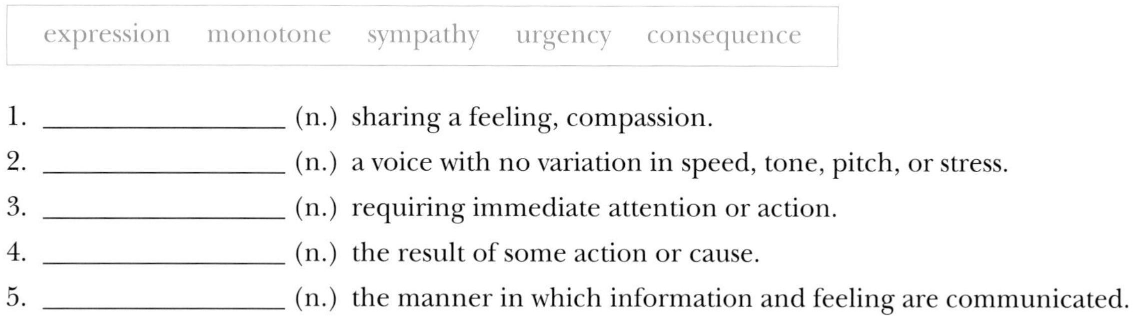

expression	monotone	sympathy	urgency	consequence

1. ______________ (n.) sharing a feeling, compassion.
2. ______________ (n.) a voice with no variation in speed, tone, pitch, or stress.
3. ______________ (n.) requiring immediate attention or action.
4. ______________ (n.) the result of some action or cause.
5. ______________ (n.) the manner in which information and feeling are communicated.

Unit 9

▶ These expressions can be used to guide the audience:

To understand my choice, you must first understand my reasons.

I hope that this explanation has clarified my choice.

Fill in the blanks with the words below.

repetition	strategy	reason	synonymous	inspire

1. ______________ (n.) a cause of action or belief.
2. ______________ (v.) to create confidence or enthusiasm in a person.
3. ______________ (adj.) words or expressions with the same meaning.
4. ______________ (n.) a plan to accomplish something.
5. ______________ (n.) doing or saying something again and again.

Unit 10

▶ These expressions may be used to introduce examples:

Perhaps an example will make things a little clearer.

An example might clarify the issue.

Look throughout Unit 10 for the words to match the definitions below.

1. ______________ (v.) to put too many things in one place.
2. ______________ (n.) uncommon language, used in specific fields.
3. ______________ (v.) to show how things are the same.
4. ______________ (v.) to show how things are different.
5. ______________ (adj.) not simple.

Unit 11

▶ Here are a few expressions you can use to introduce your opinion:

From my point of view…

Allow me to express my thoughts on the topic.

Fill in the blanks with the words below.

controversial	support	tough	position	volunteer

1. ______________ (adj.) strong or strict.
2. ______________ (n.) attitude or opinion.
3. ______________ (n.) information or evidence that confirms or explains a reason or position.
4. ______________ (n.) a person who gives time or service without pay or reward.
5. ______________ (adj.) strongly disputed matter of opinion.

Unit 12

▶ The following expressions may be used to make the transition from problem to solution:

In light of this serious problem, it is time to take a close look at possible solutions.

This problem demands our immediate attention. I'd like you to consider one possible solution.

Match each of the following key words from this unit with its part of speech and definition.

1. predict		something that can be believed or trusted.
2. memorable	adjective	to say or believe that something will happen.
3. credible	verb	enough for a particular purpose.
4. accurate	noun	special or unique, so it is easy to remember.
5. sufficient		correct or true.

Unit 13

▶ These expressions may be used to help establish empathy with the audience:

I understand how you feel about this.

I can truly appreciate how you must feel.

Look throughout Unit 13 for the words to match the definitions below.

1. ________________ (v.) to exaggerate, or claim too much.
2. ________________ (v.) to make clear or understandable.
3. ________________ (n.) decision reached after careful thought.
4. ________________ (n.) a feeling or image retained through experience.
5. ________________ (n.) the way the public regards a person.

Unit 14

▶ When introducing quotations, the following expressions may be useful:

A wise person once said…

I'd like to quote (   ), who said (   ).

Look throughout Unit 14 for words to match the definitions below.

1. ________________ (n.) a well-known phrase or sentence that offers advice or wisdom.
2. ________________ (n.) a person with special knowledge of a particular field.
3. ________________ (v.) to emphasize or draw attention to something.
4. ________________ (adj.) average, not special or talented.
5. ________________ (adj.) skilled at influencing others in an unfair way.

Unit 15

▶ The following expressions may be used to establish yourself as an impartial mediator or to compare points of view:

Both sides have legitimate claims that deserve careful consideration.

On one hand (   )/On the other hand (   )

Draw a line to match the terms on the left to its definition on the right.

1. resolve	(n.) opinions or interests that may be shared between people or groups.
2. mediate	(n.) a problem or disagreement between two people or groups.
3. dispute	(v.) to find a solution to a dispute or problem.
4. common ground	(adj.) not showing favor toward one side or the other.
5. impartial	(v.) to try to end a dispute by looking for common ground.

Unit 16

▶ The following expressions can be used to signal your conclusion or reinforce main ideas:

As this presentation draws to a close, let's review the main points.

Let's take a minute to recap the key points.

Write the part of speech and a short definition in your own words.

	part of speech	definition
1. rhetorical question	______	______________________________.
2. recap	______	______________________________.
3. reinforce	______	______________________________.
4. evaluate	______	______________________________.
5. authoritative	______	______________________________.

▶ The following expressions may be used to refer to sources for support:

Research conducted by (   ) suggests that…

Current research supports this position. A new study published by (   ) holds that…

Write the part of speech and a short definition in your own words.

	part of speech	definition
1. impromptu	______	______________________________.
2. plagiarism	______	______________________________.
3. bibliography	______	______________________________.
4. intentional	______	______________________________.
5. anxiety	______	______________________________.

このテキストのメインページ

www.kinsei-do.co.jp/plusmedia/4156

右の QR コードを読み取ると 

直接ページにジャンプできます 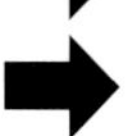

オンライン映像配信サービス「plus⁺Media」について

本テキストの映像は plus⁺Media ページ（www.kinsei-do.co.jp/plusmedia）から、ストリーミング再生でご利用いただけます。手順は以下に従ってください。

ログイン

●ご利用には、ログインが必要です。
サイトのログインページ（www.kinsei-do.co.jp/plusmedia/login）へ行き、plus⁺Media パスワード（隣ページのシールをはがしたあとに印字されている数字とアルファベット）を入力します。

●パスワードは各テキストにつき１つです。
有効期限は、はじめてログインした時点から１年間になります。

ログインページ

[利用方法]

隣ページにある QR コード、もしくは Plus⁺Media トップページ（www.kinsei-do.co.jp/plusmedia）から該当するテキストを選んで、そのテキストのメインページにジャンプしてください。

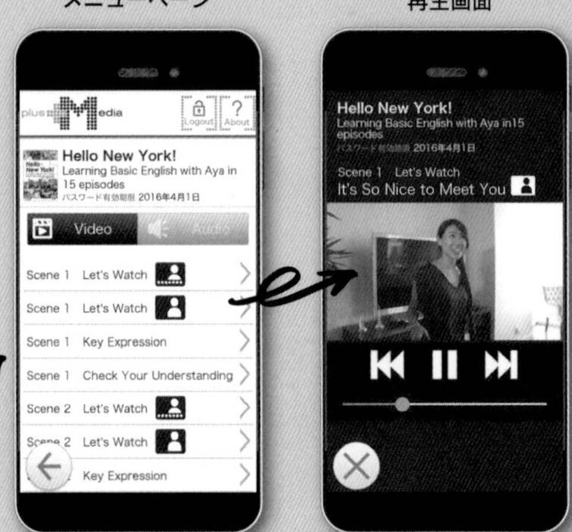

「Video」「Audio」をタッチすると、それぞれのメニューページにジャンプしますので、そこから該当する項目を選べば、ストリーミングが開始されます。

※画像はすべてイメージです

[推奨環境]

iOS (iPhone, iPad)	OS: iOS 6 ～ 13 ブラウザ：標準ブラウザ	Android	OS: Android 4.x ～ 10.0 ブラウザ：標準ブラウザ、Chrome
PC	OS: Windows 7/8/8.1/10, MacOS X　ブラウザ: Internet Explorer 10/11, Microsoft Edge, Firefox 48以降, Chrome 53以降, Safari		

※最新の推奨環境についてはウェブサイトをご確認ください。

※上記の推奨環境を満たしている場合でも、機種によってはご利用いただけない場合もございます。また、推奨環境は技術動向等により変更される場合がございます。予めご了承下さい。